# OORORME

## Pursuit of Facts

## Dr. Lalitha K. P.
### (Rashmi Nanjappa Kallichanda)

notionpress.com

INDIA · SINGAPORE · MALAYSIA

Copyright © Dr. Lalitha .K. P. 2024

All Rights Reserved.

**ISBN 979-8-89277-417-8**

# CONTENTS

# FOREWORD

Dr. K. P. Lalitha is a professor and researcher in the fields of Kannada and Folk Studies. Her works and expertise in these two fields are well known within the academic circle. She has refined her ideas through 17 long years of teaching and research. Her positive and creative personality has added a special rigor and depth to her research. Culture Studies demands a lot of hard work and commitment, and Dr. Lalitha is one of the few who chose to do it. Though she had an opportunity to have a comfortable life with a safe job, she chose the hard path of pursuing knowledge. Her friends and relatives wondered why she is choosing a difficult path to build her career. But she had a simple and straightforward answer to them, "I want to carve my identity." This answer shows that her interest in the research is coming from a deeply personal space.

Dr. Lalitha hails from Kodagu (Coorg region) situated in southern Karnataka. Though Kodagu is mostly known for its natural scenic beauty, it hosts various communities with rich cultural heritage. Dr. Lalitha wants to explore the languages, literature, culture, and traditions of the region and share them with the rest of the world. The following articles are the result of her continuing interest in the Kodagu culture.

Kodagu has attracted academic interest from the times of colonization. Many Indian and foreign scholars have researched various aspects of Kodagu. Dr. Lalitha is well aware of the previous works on Kodagu, but she wants to find her own way of understanding the subject. For the same reason, the articles in this collection are full of new perspectives.

These articles are a result of an elaborate study of the early available material on the culture of Kodagu, combined with extensive fieldwork by the scholar herself. Her analysis of the gathered material from the perspective of community, language, literature, history, women sensibilities, local belief systems and practices gives a holistic and scientific approach to these articles.

Dr. Lalitha's works showcase a deep and multi-dimensional understanding of the subject. Kodagu is popularly seen as the land of valiant soldiers and rich educated landlords. But Dr. Lalitha strives to throw light on the sixteen native tribes of Kodagu. While discussing a topic she never focuses on one community ignoring the others. She never misses an opportunity to acknowledge every tribal community with their differences and similarities. This is a sign of inclusive and sensitive research.

Another quality of Dr. Laitha worth mentioning is her courage in questioning the opinions and facts which are accepted and propagated blindly. For instance, in an article on *Pattole Palame,* the first ethnographic work on Kodagu in its native language, Dr. Lalitha praises the efforts of the author for taking up this project of recording Kodagu's folk culture on paper. But she points out that the book fails to acknowledge many of the tribes and their folk culture. For the same reason, she cautions that this popular book should not be considered to be representative of the Kodagu culture while acknowledging its historical importance. This kind of clarity comes with a commitment to an objective and truth-seeking attitude towards the subject.

It is worth appreciating that the author has given a Kannada translation of Kodava proverbs. It helps the non-native reader in understanding her analysis better. The author's observations on the scientific temperament present in some of the rituals of Kodagu, calls for our attention. An article named '*Woman in the Kodagu folklore*' is a sign of the mature scholarship of the author. Her study on local legends of Kodagu and the history of Tipu Sultan showcases her sharp analytical mind and an objective approach.

All these articles emerge from disciplined research done over a long period. The clarity of thought present in the articles is striking. Also, the articles employ a style that lends themselves to an easy read. Dr. Lalitha, with her sharp intellect and clear expression, can take Culture Studies and Kannada Studies further for good. I am looking forward to seeing more of her works in the future.

**Prof. C. N. Ramachandran**

# ACKNOWLEDGMENTS

Great reformers and scholars around the world had recognized two major reasons for the social and economic backwardness of India. The first reason was the practice of casteism. The second was the lower status of women in Indian society. India was listed as a backward country owing to its hierarchical social system and the toxic patriarchy which oppressed the women. Sadly, even in this twenty-first century, there is not much improvement as casteism and patriarchy thrive unapologetically.

Amidst all this, there was a region in India that had a social system that was radically different from the rest of the country. Kodagu is known for its natural beauty. Despite it being a small region, it has diverse languages and communities with a rich culture.

I would like to mention some of the interesting practices in the region to support my statement above. Even today, we are in a situation where a woman still has to fight for her inheritance. But in Kodagu culture, a woman enjoyed inheritance and commanded respect in the society, always. Widow remarriage was a common practice. There was no concept of dowry. The daughters of the family were never considered as a liability. Many practices, moral codes, and laws of the land in Kodagu folk culture could be considered progressive even at the global level. For example, Kodagu locals had a concept of 'Devkad', where a piece of forest land is reserved to the Gods. Humans are not allowed to tamper with it under any circumstances. There is cultural evidence that shows that the various communities in the region enjoyed equal respect and lived in harmony. I intend to analyze and understand this unique and rich culture of Kodagu with the help of folk etymology.

To someone who is lost in the mechanical urban lifestyle, memories are like an oasis in the desert. As someone who is living outside Kodagu from the last 20 and odd years, memories from my childhood often visit me. The beautiful greenery of Kodagu, the Kodava language, and the Kodava community I grew up in are alive in my memories. That particular dialect of Kodava language which my grandmother spoke; the proverbs and riddles she taught me; various festivals celebrated in the village; the answers my grandmother gave for my non-stop questions on various practices around me; different communities who were living in the village; the way the members of these communities were treated when they came to our house; the special cuisine meant for the rainy season; various food practices of different communities; multiple types of dressing that were prevalent in the village; all these memories keep visiting me. As I think about them I naturally start making mental note of things. Sometimes, these notes take the form of criticism and analysis. Gradually this process prompts me to take a pen and write them on paper. The current collection of articles is the result of this churning that happened in my head.

As we grow older to gain knowledge and experience, a few things stay with us forever. When such residues begin to pose questions, you have no option but to find answers to them. I write because it is inevitable. All these articles are the result of my constant search for answers. I am aware that all the answers I arrive at might not be correct or the absolute truth. However, I always believe that my research will inspire others to engage in seeking their own answers. To be honest, all these articles are written primarily to satisfy my curious mind. I am not here to prove the ultimate truth. I write to polish my perspective of the world around me. And I write because I believe that writing is therapeutic.

This book is called 'Oororme' for an important reason. The word 'Oororme' is used multiple times in 'Pattole Palame,' a significant ethnographic work on Kodagu by Nadikeri Chinnappa. The word refers to 'The equal respect that every community in the village deserves.' Folklore tells us that there were about thirty five native communities living in Kodagu. The word 'Oororme' acknowledges the uniqueness of each community while stating that each of them will be respected equally. The folk sources show that all the communities came together during festivals and took equal part in them. Thus, the people of Kodagu had organically enforced the idea of equality through local laws and customs. With this background, I believe 'Oororme' is most suited to be the title of this book.

All the articles in the book are based on my fieldwork in Kodagu. Every article is a result of taking part in the local festivals and rituals, personally. Also, long interviews with the locals have deepened my understanding of the subject. It was my aspiration to introduce the rich and unique culture of Kodagu to the world. So I wrote many research papers and presented them through various international journals. This book is a collection of such research papers. I sincerely thank ... and my daughter Nidhi Nanjappa for helping me bring out this book. I would like to thank all my well-wishers who have been supporting me in this pursuit. I am grateful for their love and affection.

**Dr. Lalitha K. P**

# Dr. Lalitha K. P. - Introduction

Dr. K. P. Lalitha (Rashmi Nanjappa Kallichenda), graduated from Mangalore University with the Best Student award. She got her Master's Degree from Mysore University with Gold Medals. She was awarded a Ph.D. for her thesis "Study of place names of Virajapete taluk." Karnataka Kodava Sahitya Academy, Madikeri, published her thesis as a book. As an expert on the languages in the Kodagu region, Dr. Lalitha has presented her research papers in various state, national and international seminars. Many of her research papers are published in reputed journals around the world. Considering her contribution to academics, she is presented with the National Award.Her works such as *Vivaksha, Vivechane, Jeevantha Paleyulikegala Kuritu*, and *Shodhaneya Hadiyalli* have been popular reference materials among the research students. She has also written a play 'Pommodira Ponnappa,' which is performed across the state with a good response from the audience.

K. P. Lalitha has served as the head of the Kannada department at BMS Women's College. Currently, she is working in the Kuvempu Kannada Adhyayana Samsthe, Manasa Gangothri, Mysore University.

# Life and Folklore in Coorg as seen by Nadikerianda Chinnappa

*Dr. Lalitha K. P.*

## ABSTRACT

This document gives an Analysis of life and folklore in Coorg (Kodagu), a district in Karnataka state, India on the basis of Nadikerianda Chinnappa's work called 'Pattole Palame'. In this paper an attempt has been made to discuss various aspects of life of people in Coorg as presented by Chinnappa in his work based on his observations and experience. An analysis of Social and Political Life of people in Coorg has been done with an emphasis on caste system, widow remarriage, status of women etc. All the above discussions have been done as seen by Nadikerianda Chinnappa.

**Keywords:** Coorg, Kodagu, Kodava, Pattole Palame.

## INTRODUCTION

The 'Pattole Palame' is a result of an extraordinary achievement accomplished by a common man through his common sense. This extraordinary achiever is our Nadikerianda Chinnappa. He was born in a humble Kodava family in 1875. Although he was extremely talented he stared working due to his unstable financial condition. For Chinnappa who occupied the posts of a teacher, revenue official, subedar in the army etc., the hobbies of collection and writing were his companions. As he declared, he had collected and recorded the things as he saw, heard, experienced by himself and learned from the elders. This 'Pattole Palame' is a grand record of information on the lifestyle, cultural uniqueness of the people of Coorg done in simple and appealing manner with due concern about the culture and with an aim of helping the coming generations to know their origins.

## DETAIL AND DISCUSSION

'Arnadknoorpaje' means, six 'Nadus' (regions) have hundreds of customs. The area of Coorg was divided in to Nadus (regions). In his 'Pattole Palame', Chinnappa said that such several nadus have hundreds of customs. From this, we can note that the things collected and recorded by Chinnappa may not be applicable to all Kodava people everywhere in the Coorg. It is possible that the things recorded on Kodava culture in the 'Pattole Palame' work may be applicable only to some regions or a limited area of Coorg. Supporting to this view, I would like to refer a thing said by late 'Mandeera Jaya Appana'.During 1961, the Kodava Sangha published a short form of 'Pattole Palame' work with the title: "Kodavanadap" (Kodava customs) and proclaimed the Kodava people to follow the customs, lifestyle and rules in the book. However, Kodava people didn't consider such proclamations seriously. And they didn't come forward to follow the lifestyle as said in the book.

There are reasons why Kodavas didn't respond to the Kodava Sangha and didn't follow Kodavanadap. There are differences between the customs of South Coorg and North Coorg, for example in the South Coorg region, marriage cannot be complete without the Mehandi custom (Henna) called 'Terana Beppo'. However, the people in North Coorg are not aware of this custom, which is not practiced. It is not prevalent.

There are reasons why we should not think the work 'Pattole Palame' as an ultimate representation to the Kodavas or Kodava culture. Native folklore is full of several other customs, traditions that were not recorded in this literature. However, we can proudly claim that Chinnappa attempted his best to protect the footprints of the native culture which was threatened to endangerment by the attack from the other cultures. The name of Nadikerianda Chinnappa is frontrunner among the persons who enriched the folklore of Indian Languages.

If we go back to the political and social context of the times of Chinnappa, the local officials of the Kodagu were serving the posts awarded to them by the local chieftains, and the British with honesty and quite happy with the rewards and positions assigned to them; their primary concern was to secure their positions, not the people, culture or their language and customs. With this kind of social environment, the commendable achievement was that of a common man who made big efforts to gather information on the culture he was born, lived and experienced. It must be admired that with the herculean effort, he informed and convinced the British officials about the importance of the Kodava culture and mobilised financial support for his cause and published his book with an intuitive title of 'Pattole Palame' in the year 1924.

It is important to note that there were books on Kodava culture to throw light on the lifestyle and culture of the Kodava people and they were given special place in the folklore even before the times of 'Pattole Palame'. Kodava folklore came into existence in the form of literature even before the beginning of the 19th century. To name a few, Lt. Cover's "Memories of Kodagu Survey" (1817), Dr. Mogling's "Coorg Memories", Reverend Greater's "Coorg Songs (1870)", Rictor's "Coorg Gazetteer" (1871), Holland's "Coorgs and Yeravas (1901)" works record the information on the lifestyle and customs of Coorg. However, it is significant to note that the language of the land came into life from the work 'Pattole Palame' by Nadikerianda Chinnappa. The book was an authentic record of the Kodava life by the native, in his native language and it is considered as the chef-d'oeuvre of the Kodava folklore. Since the work has taken special place among the Kodava fans, Kodava speakers, folklore experts and the likes, the book 'Pattole Palame' has seen five editions and printed in Kodava, Kannada and English languages. The first edition of the work was published in 1924 by using Kannada script with the collection of riddles, moral quotes etc. It is imperative for the readers to note before the criticism of this unique work called 'Pattole Palame' that the Chinnappa has recorded the information as a collection of things on the folklore and the culture and the information recorded were not his personal opinions on anything, therefore the author is not directly responsible for any direct criticism or reviews of his work. The work is a biggest collection of folklore for the people of his native to explore and experience the things as seen by him, and in a way it had shown the sincere efforts by the author and his great affection for the culture. This work contains an overview of the history, geographical details and complete collection of information on the customs in practice from birth to death of persons during that time. It also contains some information on the connections between the Kodavas and the tribes and communities that speak Kodava language.  The special place women had in the Kodava culture makes us to wonder today in the so called modern society.

Dowry was not practiced during those days and the society had approval for the marriage of the widows. Re-marriage was encouraged. 'Pattole Palame' contains a folk poem on the subject of a widowed woman who was married by one of the brothers of her husband.

"Choth choth chunnayi
tedigond pokane
tedi pona paballi
kal ke tore budda.
Ennanend arivira?
tannadanna devayya
kala kanda ponalli
anna bechcha momma
pandiya nadapole
ponnayi nadakalu

endenni nenatith
cheelanalla balan
baipirinji bandith
machchi manekerith
tanna petta avvang
ee suddinarpchi" [1]

*[A boy searches for a girl everywhere. However he fails to find the proper match for him. Then he realizes that the widow of his elder brother Devaih could be a proper match for him. The realization at the time seems like a medicinal herb for which he searched everywhere in the forests was just beneath the sole of his foot. He tells his mother that he wants to marry his sister in law according to the ancient customs.]*

What we see from the above, is the realisation of the Kodava culture, which had a humane approach which allowed remarriage by brother in law to give second life to a widow. It is imperative to note that the society had no negative notions about the widow marriage and remarriage during those days.

Also, according to the 'Okkaparije' and 'Makkaparije' systems as discussed in the 'Pattole Palame', when a family was devoid of a male heir, girls in the family were becoming the successors. They were allowed to marry a man to their families and run the families on their command. This shows that matriarchal system was in practice in the absence of a male heir. Also, there was a custom called 'Paitandec Alpa', which honored woman who gave birth to ten children as a 'Great Mother' by the relatives and the neighboring communities.

Several fructuous things owing to the folklore were recorded in the 'Pattole Palame' work. Also here is a description about the festivals and the collection of songs sung on the occasions. The quotes said during the 'Kail Pold' festival were as useful as experienced guidance from the elders to everyone.

Example:
> Narino pandino
> batte but panang
> shatruna enangate
> mittoorak toneyayinil
> rayang miniyate
> devala mareyate

*[Tiger and wild boars should be hit out of their path. Do not anger the enemy. Be helpful to your friends. Never go against the King. Do not forget the god.]*

The words such as above which teach the values of life to all are relevant even till this date. The folk songs sung during childbirth, marriage, death are recorded in the original Kodava language.

Along with the above, an analysis is needed on the caste system discussed in the 'Pattole Palame' work.The castes other than Kodava are considered as 'Shudra' in the 'Pattole Palame' work. The castes related to the same can be listed as follows:

The Shudras of the Teeyas, Billavas, Peggades, Airies, Bannas, and Agasas should not be allowed in the nellakki nadubade, kannikombare and kitchen sections of the Kodava houses. [1]

Medas, Holeyas, Martas and the castes of similar levels should stand on the yard. [1]

It is inevitable that the above things will confuse the readers. The author has recorded few quotes in the miscellaneous section of the next pages. One quote is as follows:

"Pole movane talemovan", means the Son of the Dalit caste is the elder son of our family. The elders might have the knowledge of the love, care, respect and the responsibility lay on the shoulders of the elder son. It says, "even if the Holy Scriptures is wrong, wise sayings can never be wrong". It is not understood though, when they consider Dalit boy the elder son of their family, why they called their elder son 'Shudra' and kept him beyond the reach of their household.

There is another wise saying recoded in the 'Pattole Palame', regarding the 'Meda' community. "Pani ariyatha moodina medang kodkondu" which means the girl who doesn't know how to carry out the household chores should be married to the boy of the Meda community.

On this occasion also, if the elders of the local culture thought that 'Meda' community as untouchable, how did they think about the girl from their household to be married to the boy? No, not at all. The above lines express the concern, respect and their confidence about the sincerity and appreciation they have had about the skills of the people of that community, and not the feeling that they are Shudras/Untouchables.

There were 17 communities in the Coorg that were identified as tribals of Coorg who followed Kodava language, culture, lifestyle and identified them as the natives of Kodagu from several years, even before the publishing of 'Pattole Palame'. Western scholar Richtor recorded 23 communities as the speakers of Kodava language. It is possible that all the communities which were identified as the natives had lived a life of harmony. It is a culture which sheltered each community who extended their helping hand to one another.

There are supporting information in the history of Coorg and native folklore which help me conclude this way. Richtor records in his writings that the Mark Cubbon, the then British commissioner, in his order, didn't consider the people of Coorg as an ethnicity or race, instead he considerd them as gallant people of Coorg and calls them as little nation of warriors, and provides them exception from the anti-arms act prevalent at those times.

The history reveals that the erstwhile Kings who ruled Coorg considered the people here as Kodava people and used them for their services. The Hunsur inscription, which was the first ever inscription, makes reference of the Coorg and calls them as 'Ella naada kodavaru'. The culture had no recognition for the hierocracy and the clergy class. The folklore culture identified and respected its elders as their 'Karonas' (origin) and worshipped them and were grateful them.

Most importantly, the folklore culture and its elders showed affection, respect, and devotion towards the people who helped them regardless of the communities they belonged to. They showed their gratitude in the form of providing them residence in their places.

A person named Katal Boltu who belonged to the Kapala Dalit community was dearest among the friends of Ponnappa a folklore warrior who was famous in the name of Kalyatajjappa. 'Pattole Palame' includes the collection of a poem in which the historical details of 'Katalbolthu' sacrificing his life for his friend were mentioned. The natives still show their gratitude to 'Katalbolthu' by providing him 'Ede' (sacrificial meal offered to the deity) and in a village called Ponnampete, an elderly person who belongs to 'Kembatti Holeya' community takes the center stage in the religious traditions and festivities and the native Kodavas respect him with devotion. When a Dalit priest is apotheosised with a God called 'Poladeva' during the 'Badrakali' festival at the Nadikeri village, there is a custom where all the Kodava devotees salute him by touching his feet and get Prasada from him.

From the examples above, it can be understood that the concept of Kodava culture could be very recent. The lifestyles of all but 17 communities who are natives of Coorg should come under the concept of Kodava ethos. There may not have been any class systems in the original culture. The outsiders identified these people as Kodavas, who lived with their different hereditary professions. It can be supposed that the vested interests might have divided the society on the later days.

For example, it can be supposed that the people who took major occupations such as growing the 'Kembutti Bhatta' (Red Raddy) were called as 'Kembatti Holeyas', people who made baskets, fans, punnets and receptacles etc. were called 'Medas', the people who were experts in haircutting were called 'Nayindas' and the people who determined auspicious and inauspicious moments for the festivities and the important occasions in life were called 'Kaniyas'. Then their roles and positions in the society may be determined based on the same.

There is no ambiguity that the social classifications were made long before the time of 'Pattole Palame' and Chinnappa has handed over the things he saw, experienced, and heard to the next generation in a sincere manner. However, the research of the original culture that was prevalent since long time needs to be done.

A grass-root research work needs to be taken up in a scientific manner to bring the folklore of the land to the light. Each village and street across the Kodagu should be researched and the collection of the oral folklore needs to be done. An attempt should be made to research the source of the local culture by threading the path of this oral folklore. Conceptual discussions on the culture should take place for the same purpose. It is possible that such conceptual discussions will help getting clear picture of the culture.

A collection of the folklore needs to be done in conceptual manner without negligence and considering any aspect of the local society as mean.

## CONCLUSION

'Pattole Palame' book is not the only yardstick of the Kodagu ethos. It is a genuine effort of collecting information reflecting the culture and traditions of a community. We need to put our sincere efforts to discover the original culture based on the 'Pattole Palame' work and while returning to our roots, we should be able to spread the flavors of this rich heritage to the entire world.

## REFERENCES


[1] Nadikerianda Chinnappa, Pattole Palame, Karnataka Sahitya Academy, Madikeri, p. 131, 538, 539.

[2] D. N. Krishnaih, History of Coorg, Prasaganga, University of Mysuru.

[3] Ephigraphiya Karnatika Kodagu Jille – Volume 1, Kannada Adhyayana Samsthe, University of Mysuru.

[4] Dr. P.S. Ramanujam, Kodavaru, Prasaranga, Mysuru, 1975.

[5] Chief editor Hampana, Aimamuttanna, Kodava Kannada Nighantu, Karnataka Sahitya Parishattu, Bengaluru.

[6] Edited by Tambanda Vijay Poonachcha, Kodagu Vivarane, Prasaranga, Kannada University, Hampi.

[7] V.N. Nayak, Kodagina Bhougolika Sameekshe, Deepak Prakashana, Goni Koppalu, South Kodagu.

[8] Edited by N.S. Devi Prasad, Kodaginalli Bhasha Samskritika Samarasya, Amara Kranti Utsava Samiti, Sulia, Dakshina Kannada.

[9] Chief editor Baragooru Ramachandrappa, Upa Samskriti Adhyayana Maaleya Pustakagalu, Karnataka Sahitya Academy, Nripatunga Road, Bengaluru.

[10] Tambanda Vijay Poonachcha, Adhunika Kodagu.

# Kallu Botis (Stone Pillars) in Kodagu

*Dr. Lalitha K. P.*

The history of kodagu, a small district on the south- west of Karnataka is very amazing. It is interesting as well as curious to learn that, the 'KALLUBOTI's, which are a part of specifically particular folk culture of this area also provide us the historical evidences, like other inscriptions on stones, palaces, 'Kadanga's, 'Kaimada's and structures, which are the living proofs of the history of this district.

## KALLUBOTI's

The description regarding these 'KALLUBOTIs are available to us in the folk literature of this area.

> 'Pattik chingaara kallraboti
> Manika kallond kejjapaniyo
> Chomana talatuva kaggalboti
> Chomana kattuva kaggalboti
> Pare kalkond kejja paniyo' .

This can be roughly translated as;
> Stone pillar is a decoration to the frontal space
> Built in beautiful stone
> This pillar is to harness the unruly cow
> This pillar is also used to tie the cow
> Around that, there is a stony frontal
> Beautifully spacious stoned quadrangal.

Lines above in the folk culture of Kodagu emphasize the beauty and the usage of these 'kalluboti's.

These 'kalluboti's are found in the houses constructed by the ancestors, which are called 'ainmane' and in the paddy hives. Though, these are found normally on the east or on the south-east of 'ainmane', it is also found placed in the paddy hives, which were used to harvest the paddy crop during the season, stands as a technical connect of the traditional culture of the 'kodava's harvesting culture.

The pillars or the 'Kalluboti's found near the harvesting area, are usually made of either stone or wood, measuring about four feet tall and with a circumference of about six feet. These pillars found in the quadrangles of 'Ainmane' are normally made of stones. these are called 'chitrakal boti' and 'attakal boti'. Even  today, one can find these pillars in the ancestral houses of 'ainmane's belonging to 'Bachiraniyanda' family house and 'Kallangada' family house in virajpet taluk and till recently, in the ancestral 'ainmane's of 'kollira' family house in 'kalatmad' village in Gonikoppa of virajpet thalukthese 'kalluboti's were seen.

Normally, 'chitrakal boti's are 5 to 9 feet tall. Either they will be round or will have 8 or 16 faces. Blossomed lotus, star, snake hood, creepers birds and the likes are carved on these faces, The top of the pillars will either be made to look like a tower or a pot. This can be seen in 'Bacharaniyanda' family 'Ainmane' primises.

In contrast to this, on the top of the pillars of 'attakal boti', ox ie, 'Basava' is sculpted. This type of 'attakal boti's, which are decorated with ox sculpture ie, 'Vrishabha' or 'Basava', are found in 'Ainmane's belonging to 'Kaibulira' family house of 'Tavalageri', 'Kollira' family house in 'Kalatmad' village and also in other 'Ainmane's and paddy hives, belonging to many other family houses as well.

These are all, of course, the overview to the descriptions of the pillars or the 'Kallubotis'.

The idea of this present article is to analyze the historical details behind these pillars having the ox ie, 'Basava' sculpture carved on these 'Attakal botis' found in various places of KoDagu. Here is an attempt to analyze the background of these 'Attakal botis', from the opinions expressed by the locals, which I had come across, while I was on a field work pertaining to the study of 'Stalanaama" or the place name studies.

These 'Attakal botis' are found in large numbers in the village of 'Kalatmad', near Gonikoppa of virajpet taluk in southern Kodagu. Ox ie, 'Basava' sculptured pillars are found in the quadrangles and paddy hives in the local households of this area. Of course, Not seen nowadays.

It has been found understandably  that, because of the presence of these 'attakal botis' only, this village received its name as 'Kalatmad  or 'Kalathle maad.  The word 'KaLatmad' is originally a word derived from Malayalam language. In malayalam, 'KaLa' means harvesting area and 'Maad' means the cattle. Hence,  the word 'Kalatmad'.means Basava idol in the harvesting area.

The history of these 'Kallubotis' are so powerful as to influence the village to derive its name after it, is so exiting and can also throw light on the life style to unravel the history of the bygone era.

Kodagu, under the rule  of  veerashaivas of Haleri dynasty, who were very powerful. To express their loyalty to the  rulers, the then seniors of this village had shown respect to the religion of the ruler also, by installing these pillars with the 'Basava' ie, the ox sculpture in their quadrangles and in their paddy hives. There are instances of receiving special benefits and rewards from the rulers for doing so. Here is an account to substantiate the same.

Every kodava Family has a specific name attached to it, which are called 'okkapada'. During the reign of the Haleri dynasty rule, there is a family called 'Kollira'.  As per the orders of the king, this 'kollira' family engaged themselves in executing the order by punishing those who went against the king, thereby getting the patronage of the king, They were even killing people of their own community. Thus their families were called 'Kollira' family. In the local language 'koll' means kill, it was picturesquely explained the local.

Even today we can find such 'Attakal boti's in front of the 'Ainmane's of the 'Kollira' family houses, as a mark of proof of this local elderly person's remarks and in comparison to the land holdings of the rest of the families in this village, this 'Kollira' families have larger land holdings.

That goes to show that, the helpless and selfish motives of the locals, who bowed down to the rulers from outside, at the cost of sacrificing their own culture and originality.

If we look at the history, we gather more information in support of this subject. This district has a cultural history, which spreads to over 2500 years. Initially, it appears that, the 'Chengalvas' sowed the seeds of 'veerashaivism in Kodagu. We find many such stone sculptures of 'Basava' in many places in Kodagu, although, many are disfigured and many are destroyed. Hence we can deduce that, In the later years, the rulers of the 'Haleri' dynasty effectively spread the Veerashaiva Dharma in entire Kodagu. There is no room for suspicion that, these 'Basava' idols represent the existence of veerashaiva religion here.

We do not come across any presence or the influence of Veerashaiva Dharma in the cultural life of the oboriginal kodava s. The locals worship gods like Kaveri, Iggutppa, Bhadrakaali, Aynadeva and demons like Kuttichatha, Chavundi, Pashanamoorthy.

It is said that, Aynadeva is an incarnation of lord Shiva or Eeshwara. May be so. But, interestingly, we do not find any sculpcture or idol of Basava in these centers of Aynadeva.

Instead of that, we find, 'Botekaara' or the pochar in the form of dogs, made out of mud are seen. But in Mahadeva temples one can see the stone idols of Basava. Mahadeva, in fact is not a word found in kodava language at all. This has to be pondered over. Mahadeva is seen as a symbol of kannada language and other culture. The original kannada word 'Mahadeva' has undergone dialectical changes in accordance with the Kodava language dialect, by losing its long resonance in the second letter and combining with the first word 'Maha' to become 'Maadeva' in common usage. Probably, these "Mahadeva' temples came in to existence during the reign of either 'Chengaalvas' or 'Haleri' dynasties is a possibility. we cannot deny the fact that the 'Cholas, who ruled Kodagu during the 11 century were shaivites.

Similarly, if we take a look at the reign of 'Haleri' dynasty, we have a long list of fourteen kings that ruled here, including a queen's rule. As for the verity of political history and history of conflicts are considered, the rule of Siribayi Doddveerappa, Dodda Veera Rajendraodeya, Eradane Lingarajendra odeya and Chikka Veera Rajendra odeya, have all contributed considerably to make it interesting.

Kings hailing from 'Haleri' dynasty have ruled Kodagu from the last part of the 16th century till the early part of 19th century.

If we observe the cultural history of Kodagu, many dynasties that ruled over Kodagu, have directly or indirectly influenced the local culture. It will not be wrong to say that, specially the administration of 'Haleri' dynasty has considerably made its mark on the cultural and social life of common people, both progressively as well as disastrously.

Although, The ideals, the struggle and the way of mingling with the locals, of certain 'Haleri' kings, have contributed to the betterment of the locals, on the other hand, it will not be an exaggeration to say that, the blind love about their mother tounge 'Kannada' and unstinted faith about their Veerashaiva Dharma had made them employ harder controls on the religious and social liberties of the locals life.

As kannada was made the official language, during their tenure of administration, local languages like kodava and other local dialects were forced to a corner. Language of the subjugated could not have been the administrative language at all. It is very surprising to note that, the original settlers, who are by nature  are strong fighters and intelligent seldom tried to assume power themselves or administrate their own land, rather succumbed to the aggression, power and administration of the outsiders. Excepting a few, no one is seenin the history, holding the absolute power or taking the administration to their hands.

History bluntly showcases to us that, the locals were more concerned in protecting their personal interests by bowing down to the rulers, than trying to protect their own people, their own culture, their own land and language.

Veerashaiva culture was never a practice of any sect of the koDava original settlers. But, in a hurry to please the ruling 'Haleri' dynasty, to prove their loyalty to them and to receive rewards and benefits,  The installetion of the above discussed 'Kallubotis' in their quadrangals and in their hives is a glaring example of the plight of the locals.

There obviously rises a question that, if in case the local settlers carried away by the teachings of Veerashaiva Dharma and subjected themselves willingly to it, why are we seeing these defaced or dilapidated pillars carrying the sculptures of Basava idols all around us now? Whereas, various ancient temples spread all around koDagu are in commendably good condition under the careful concern of the locals.

---

The reason is obvious. The locals either in order to please the rulers or may be with an intention to be under the patronage of the ruler or even may be to avoid the adverse effect of going against the ruler, may have installed the pillars of ie the 'Kallubotis', who although despised the Veerashaiva Dharma, pretended to adore or express their devotion to it, seem to be opportunists. Or even we can deduce that, maybe the helplessness to show their resistance to the oppressive rule of the king and the administrative system of the day.

# Cultural History of Kodagu

*Dr. Lalitha K. P.*

Culture denotes refinement of mind and manners. Culture is the soul of the people, the basic beliefs, attitudes, and spiritual values that have become their way of life. It is a source of both mental delights and physical comforts; it makes one forget the crudities of the external world; it creates a refined taste; and more than everything else, Kodava culture enables a Kodava to harmonize differences. Customs have generally accepted conventions that are put into practice consistently and devotedly, and those practices gradually become a part and parcel of what is called culture. Cult or cultivate, is an act of development, a conventional process, an individual or social discipline, etc. Rituals observed, the system of worship, traditional values, manners, social conduct, language or dialect, a certain pattern of customs, names, etc, form different roots and branches of the tree-called culture. Similarly, songs, hymns, classics, and all kinds of literary" out-put are scripture.

The people of Kodagu have evolved a distinctive culture through the ages. The Paat style in poetry is the unique feature of Kodava literature. Kodavas had inherited culture and were endowed with refined tastes right from their birth. There is no need for them to go abroad to acquire culture. KodavaPaat holds a mirror to life. There can be no better means of understanding the mind of people than a careful study of their words, idioms, and proverbs. The culture of the Kodavas enables them to practice simple piety, to honor parents and elders, touching their feet thrice, to tolerate religious diversity, to lead a life of virtue and to give much with grace - Balliyamanasluemaapmaadi. The Ain-manae, Ambala, Mand and Parmb were centres of cultural activity. Noble principles were imbibed along with the mother's milk. The mother's advise to the child "Construct tanks, sink wells, plant trees, cultivate the land, wipe the tears of the affected and protect your followers and country. (as soon as a Kodava woman delivers a male child, a burning ball is shooted towards the sky fixing it to the bow and arrow, after introduction of gun culture, a gum is fired in the air to announce his birth, then a bow and arrow made from the veins of a castor plant is placed in the baby's hands, symbolic of the martial traditions of the Kodavas)

The most part of the history of Kodaga are in the form of "PAAT style"with complete picture or story of the event or person or deity. Some of such PAAT are 1) Deshaqattpaat, (description of the land and how it was administered.) 2) Kaaveripaat, (the story of Kaaveri) 3) Thottpaat(lullabies) 4) Makkadapaat (Nursery Rhymes) 5) Battaepaat, (song for the way) 6) Mangalapaat (wedding song) 7) NariMangalapaat (song for Nari marriage-after killing a tiger) 7) Chaavupaat ( funeral song) 8) Polchhipaat, (song in praise of the dead person from birth to death and praying the God to send the dead persons soul to heaven) 8) Devadapaat (songs of Gods and Goddesses) 9) and songs of Heroes.

Kodava culture like other societies consists of Proverbs, old sayings, riddles, beliefs and superstitions. There are more than 760 proverbs.

Kodava folk-arts, folk songs and dances came out of the hearts of those simple people in natural way of the day's gone-by. These folk —arts such as songs, dances, fables, and ballads left by the ancient poets who lived within their own small environment, are still admired and held in high esteem. During ancient and medieval period Kodavas did not know to read and write and were out of the literary world, and indeed Kodava language had no script.

In those yet unrecorded manners of speaking of the ancestors, one could see the wealth of wisdom and knowledge of people who expressed or sung them extempore. What had thus begun in the hoary past, were passed on for generations in unconventional ways, That is our rich intellectual heritage. In their traditional festivities, weddings and social and religious ceremonies or celebrations, one could still find a lot of well-thought — out ancient precepts and practices prevailing. They sang the song of the universe; they prayed for the humanity and they worshipped Mother- Earth. They also knew about the stars and planets, and many more things without even going to an elementary school. Their knowledge was admirable. They knew about the seven seas and seven continents and fourteen worlds. They knew about the illusive heaven and hell. These things together enriched Kodava lives, human values and ethics.

These are the people, the Kodavas, who fostered a way of life for centuries, living away in the hillside and plains as hunters and agriculturists. They had and still have their own traditional dress, very colourful and dignified. The Kodava race is after all a part and parcel of India's ethnic mosaic. Their folklore too carry the same views and spirits of what those elsewhere in India had said and sung, but the art and beauty of the folklore of Kodavas lie in its abundant charm, originality and profound melody. Whatever their functions or ceremonies the song (baalopaat) begins thus;

> Baalo. .. baalo. . . nangada. . .
> Deva..baalo. . .Madeva. . ..
> Devi... baalo. .. Madevi. . ..
> Patta. . . baalo. .. Suuriya. . .
> Kuuda. . .baalo. . .Channuura. ..
> Bhuumi. . .baalo. . ..]abbuumi. ..

All the kodava ballads begin with these words, and those are symbolic of their noble sentiments and poetic rituals. Every aspect of the Kodava folk—songs seem lovely because those lines depict simple truth in a flowing style.

Whatever experiences they had, spoke out in the form of songs from the depth of their hearts. They seemed to have been very much accomplished individuals. From line to line they blurted out the song without any prior thoughts or notes, revealing their intellectual prowess. All ballads of Kodavas may be related to festivals, wedding, death etc. and this continues in a greater detail till date. What is interesting to note is that the song flows effortlessly, often spiced with beautiful similies and aptly used idioms in just a dialect that was spoken by hardly one lakh and odd people. The Kodavafimeral (chaavupaat and polchipaat) song is certainly poetic and philosophic from beginning to end., with beautiful similies and metaphors the song inspires every feeble heart, and the poetry is true to life. Kodava folk-songs consists of a good many worldly truths, and those words and rhythms freely collide as the cane sticks clatter all over the Kodaguhorizon.The big-bang drums, the blowing of trumpets and pipes, the clattering of the cane sticks, all fill the air, and throughout the jungles and fields, hills and dales of the land that was once a home of exclusively the Kodavas for many centuries.

The folklores, folk-songs and folk-dances are generally thought- provoking. There's nothing that could be ignored in these nor considered as insigni?cant. Those spontaneous pioneers who created the wealth of folklores, folk-arts, dances etc. were certainly the greater thinkers greater than the modern men and women who seem to be intellectually bankrupt and super?uous. In that way those anonymous creators of these folklores and folk-arts live longer and for generations in the hearts of people. At present some folk- arts and folklores are recorded, but some are not because they are out of mind and out of practice.

# A few notes on the tribal community Malekudiya

*Dr. Lalitha K. P.*

India is a multicultural country. This country has found unity in diversity. Numerous tribes have enriched the culture of India through their unique traditions and practices. This article talks about one such tribe known as Malekudiya. The following article presents a few facts derived from a study based on scientific methods.

Malekudiya has been an important tribe in the state of Karnataka. This tribe is known for its unique cultural practices. Despite the limited population of this tribe, the members have managed to maintain their cultural identity intact. Even in modern times, the community has upheld its traditional practices and cultural identity. The tribe often resides in the hilly areas of Kodagu, South Canara, and Chikkamagaluru. In Kodagu, the tribe is referred to as Kuidya. In South Canara, it is referred to as Malekudiya and in Chikkamagaluru it is called Malaikudi or Maleya.

The tribe takes its name from two Dravidian words Male and Kudi. Male means hill and Kudi means children. Thus Malekudiya simply means Children of Hills, as they have been primarily residing in the hilly areas for ages. Though they are referred by different names in different regions, all the names mean the same. Some such names are Malekudiyaru, Kudiyaru, Maleyan, Kudiyan Goudar, Kudiya, Malaikudi, Malekudi, Malekudiya. According to the recent census, the population of the tribe is 7,704.

Malekudiya tribe is spread along the Western Ghats, from Agumbe to Brahmagiri. The tribe is usually divided into two different clusters. One cluster is called Nalku Malekudiya and the other is called Mooru Malekudiya.

Nalku Malekudiya cluster is in the South Canara region. The prefix refers to the four hills on which the Malekudiya tribe lives (Nalku means four). These hills are called Barimale, Panjaru Male, Ambottamale, Elimale. Muru Malekudiya cluster is in the Kodagu region. Muru means three and it refers to the three hills on which the tribe lives. These hills are called Poomale, Themale, and Oomale. Currently, no member of the Oomale community is found. Interestingly, there is modern nomenclature for one particular community of the tribe, who left the hills to work in the areca nut farms. They are called as Adike Kudiya (Areca nut Kudiya).

All these names usually refer to the regional and linguistic identities of the tribe. For example, in Kodava language, Kudiya means family. And a particular community of the tribe lived in a forest called Poomale. Hence the community was called Poomale Kudiya.

The mother tongue of Poomale Kudiya is Kodava language. But they can speak Kannada and Tulu also. Their original occupation is extracting toddy from the local variety of palm tree (Baine Mara). Since many of the traditional practices of Poomale Kudiya are as same as that of the Kodava community, they are considered to be the original inhabitants of the region. This tribe has various Okkas or clans within. These okkas are formed based on various deities, ancestors, local gods, and localities.

In South Canara, the Malekuidya tribe is found in Beltangadi, Sulya and Karkala taluks which are situated along the Western Ghats.

Some of the hills where the Malekudiya tribe lives include Elori Male and Sidya Male of Sulya taluk. The tribe lives on the high hills in the vicinity of the villages like Munjade, Charmadi, Kayarpadi, Hatyadka, Shibaje, Shishila, Kokkala, Pudubetta, Kananja, Dharmasthala, Sidle, Patrame, Naravi, Neriya, Navuru, and Malavanthike.

Many more Malekudiya habitats are found in Kallache of the village Munjade, Annaru of Charmadi, Moodaladu of Hatyadka, Bandihali of Shivaje, Badigudde of Shishila, Perikolli, Meretadka, Gudde Thota, Kattada Bayalu of Dharmasthala, Ambe Majalu, Alangayi of Neriya, Gandibagilu, Kandanje, Elimale, Panjaru Male, Ambotti Male, Mallara Pallu, Elaneeru, Kariyaalu, Periyadka.

Malekudiya tribe forms 34.15% of the total population of Belthangadi. Many of the tribe members have agricultural lands. They are leading a sustainable life by growing various crops including coconut, areca nut, banana, black pepper, elaichi, and rice. Only 7.77% of the Malekudiya live on the hills.

The major community of Malekudiya found in Kodagu is Poomale Kudiya. The community is situated in Yavakapadi, Jodupalu, Galibeedu, Bettattooru, Naladi Total Colony, Naladi Mekekoppa Colony, Onachalu, Devarakolli, Koynadu, Nadyamale, and Madegrama.

As much as 100 to 120 Kudiya families are found in the villages of Kammadi of Temalekudiya, Kattappalli, Jodupaalu, Devarakolli, Madenadu, Karajakotu, Eravali, Kanagandi, Garemure, Madat Male, Karikepongana Colony, Karikekolangare Colony, Karike Attakere Colony, Karike Kudiyangala Colony, Karike Mundesthana Colony. Around seventy families of Adike Kudiya are found in the villages Arekallu, Guddegadde, and Kuntathikana.

Malekudiya tribe is thought to be living in an abundance of forest resources. But, in reality, the members are far from having a comfortable life. Like most other tribes, Malekudiya too is devoid of basic necessities. The people are leading a life of poverty. They have no land of their own except for the land on which their houses stand. Though they have lived in the forests all along, they can't have a claim on forest land. Many tribes like Koraga, Baitara, Mansa have lived in caves by hunting animals for centuries together. Though the rest of the world embraced modernity, these tribes never got a chance to change their lifestyle. While the rich of South Canara own farmlands and thus grow only richer, Malekudiya people end up work in their farms as laborers.

## Changing social and economic conditions of the Malekudiya

Change is the law of nature. It is inevitable. Human society is no exception to this law. The communities which were considered to be conservative are becoming modernized. We can safely say that India as a country has changed a lot in the last twenty years. This process of change continues even further and in the next twenty years, India might go through many radical changes.

These examples might prove that the country has gone through many important changes. Earlier the villages were economically and socially backward. There was no communication media. Life revolved around agriculture. The agricultural products were sold through local markets. But there was a danger of getting conned by the middlemen. Poverty was the norm. Diseases were treated with indigenous methods with the help of herbal medicines. People got married at a young age and became parents early on in their lives. The average life expectancy was less. People lived in joint families. Newspapers, radio, television were just fiction for the villagers.

But today, village life is transformed completely. Most of the villages are well connected through roads. The villages are connected to towns and cities better than ever before. People can leave for the city in the morning and return home in the evening conveniently. People are finding occupations in various fields apart from agriculture. The farmers are now capable of selling their products in the taluk or district centers for a fair price.

Schools are open in most of the villages and the younger generation is getting educated at a faster pace. As a result, superstition and oppressive practices are getting obsolete. People are finding livelihood in business, services, and industries. Hence the villages have grown dependant on the cities. The villagers are now getting finances through cooperative banks. This has freed them from the oppressive methods of the money-lending class of the village. With the availability of modern medicine, the infant mortality rate has reduced. The average age of marriage has increased. Newspapers and television are now ubiquitous in the villages. The villages have become a place of many activities. Caste dynamics have changed. The oppressive caste system is weakening. Democracy has reached the villages through local governing bodies. The state of the poor has gotten better. The list goes on.

Coming back to the subject of this study, Kodagu and South Canara are predominantly agrarian regions. Hence people from the Malekudiya tribe in both these regions are involved in agriculture as laborers. But they continue their traditional occupations such as hunting and collecting micro products from the forests.

Some of the members of the tribe are found to be employed in the public sector also. Some are into tailoring, beedi making, and shopkeeping. Some are involved with commercial crops. Animal husbandry is considered to be the original profession of Malekudiya. Despite all this, we don't see Malekudiya people owning expensive vehicles like Jeeps and Cars. Only a few of their houses have scooters and bicycles.

Since the natural habitat of Malekudiya was dense forests, the members of the tribe made their living by collecting micro products from those forests. Roots and tubers were their staple food. Their hunting skills too helped to fill their stomach. Every day, they consumed the toddy extracted from a local palm tree called Baine Mara. They were skilled at weaving baskets and collecting honey, which provided a source of income.

But today they are considering agriculture, animal husbandry, pig farming, and agricultural labor for their livelihood. Those who are educated are employed in Government institutions. They are believing less in the superstitions which are prevalent in the community, and they are slowly progressing in society. There is a noticeable improvement in their social and economic status.

***

# Women in Kodagu's Folklore

*Dr. Lalitha K. P.*

The district of Kodagu, though small in size, has made a mark for itself in the whole world due to its unique culture. It serves to illustrate the Kannada proverb "Short in physique, yet greatly famous". A repository of folklore, literature and culture, Kodagu is home to many communities which are regarded as native inhabitants. The mother-tongue of all these communities is Kodava. They practice rituals and customs that are in league with Kodava culture, and they come under the ambit of Kodava folklore. In addition to these communities, there are a few tribal communities living here, such as  Erava, Kuruba, Malekudiya etc. The culture of all these communities, in sum, can be considered as Kodava culture.

There are many proverbs, riddles and folk songs about women of the Kodava society in the folklore of Kodava language. They show in a beautiful manner the position, respect, honour, regard, affection and concern that women have had in local culture. 'Pattole Palame', the first text of Kodava folk literature, has references to Kodava women and their courage.

The text states that a Kodava woman who killed a 'tiger' earned the honour of 'hulimaduve' (to be contextualised): "When men kill a tiger, they must tie an oja (a piece of red cloth) to the rifle, and when women kill a tiger, they must tie an oja to their head".

These lines draw our attention to the valour of Kodava women. They had the courage, ingenuity and skill needed to kill a tiger. We come to know from the history of the Kodavas that the ruler Chikkaveerarajendra had formed an army of women during his reign. Women soldiers too were made to perform drills that men soldiers performed. It is mentioned in the section of the gazette related to Kodagu that the king used to take the army of women when he went on outings. Chikkaveerarajendra, for sure, must have had an idea of the capability of these women. Therefore, he formed the army of women and deployed them in day patrolling and hunting. This is corroborated by the following folk song:

Kaalakaliyugathikkamaayi Kaalakaliyuganaanikkakane AanpadepoppadmahalokathullaPongapadepopadkannaarek ande

I am seeing the magic of Kaliyuga;
It is common for an army of men soldiers to go to war.
But, I am witnessing the surprising sight
Of an army of women marching to war.

These lines make it clear that the king put the army of women to good use.

There are many proverbs in the folk literature of Kodava language that talk about the greatness, the ideals and the honour of Kodava women. Some of them are as follows;

- Badavandallinjaponnkondabakkondu;
  Balyavandaokkakkponnkodkondu.
- Raajyakkbalyavanedore;Avvanabechavaneappa.
- Ponnalkpolevaadille;Pallenaaikbattille.
- Avvanillathakunjiyu male illathaboleyuonde .
- Avvanundegiappanundillengiappakollikaneke.
- Avvachathakkaappachikkappa .
- Avva errand chaaku; Appakettimaaru.
- Pori chothaethnaneekudikulpondu;
  Kejjichothapongalapaakudikulpondu.
- Avvanda mole kudichithdumbathakela;
  Appandaberaoothithdumbuvaa?

---

* A girl from a poor family must be brought in marriage. A girl should be given in marriage to a rich family.

* The king is the greatest one in a kingdom. One who takes care of his mother is a real father.

* Fines are not imposed on women.
  A she-dog participating in hunting does not get a share of the game.

* A child without its mother and a crop without rain are the same.

* A father is valued only when there is a mother; otherwise, he is like a firebrand.

* When a mother dies, the father becomes a younger uncle.(to be contextualised)

* A mother feeds her children even by begging. A father sells his children to anyone.

* Oxen that are tired after ploughing fields must be taken to a place where there is water. Women who are exhausted after toiling must be relieved of their tiredness by offering milk.

* Will the stomach that does not become full with mother's milk become full by sucking the father's thumb?

Many proverbs like the ones above express the importance of a mother and the love, concern and respect that women have had in the family and the society.

The role of the mother is of a high standard within the family. A mother is given respect, recognition and regard in every aspect. She is given special respect during the marriage of her children. She is entitled to such respect even if she has entered another family after remarriage, or even if she is a widow.

A groom prays to god and, immediately after doing so, he offers his respects at the feet of his mother. This is mentioned in a folk song summarised as follows:

After praying to his ancestors, a groom bends down and touches the feet of his mother by way of offering his respect to her and seeks her blessings. The souvenir given by the mother as a token of her blessings must be considered a special object and preserved carefully by a bride or a groom.

During the marriage ceremony, the mother of the bride ties pattak – a consecrated string considered auspicious – to the neck of her daughter, instead of the groom tying the taali to the bride as practised among other communities. The mother of a son offers a gold chain named pommaale to him during an auspicious occasion. The woman who becomes a mother-in-law welcomes her daughter-in-law with utmost affection by offering rice mixed with sugar and milk. Even the son-in-law offers rice mixed with sugar and milk, and shows respect and love to his mother-in-law.

Elders of the community say that a woman who begot ten children was honoured with the title Mahataayi and a special ritual named Paitandekalpamangala was performed to show respect to her. The ritual was celebrated on a grand scale like a wedding.

The members of the natal family of the mother are also shown respect. During occasions such as marriages, a special ritual named Balebirudemba is performed to show respect to the members of the natal family of the mother. The maternal uncle is held in high esteem.

Just as the head of the family is called koravukaara, his wife is called koravokaarti, indicating that both of them are shown equal respect.

The ancestors of a lineage are deified and small shrines named kaimada are built for them. They are worshipped in the gurukaarona method. On such occasions, the elderly women of the lineages are also paid great respect. For example, Karanacchi's kaimada (shrine) is located in the household of Madreera family of Kunda village in Virajapete taluk. An elder of the family gave the information that when Doddaveera Rajendra Wodeyar was in prison, all the members of Madreera family perished due to Tippu Sultan's invasion. Only a girl child survived, and she was brought up by the Teetamaada family. They made her the makkaparije (an inheritor of a lineage), and established that she had the right over the lands of the Madreera family. Therefore, she became the preceptor kaaranacchi to the family.

Similarly, Halligattu village's Mookalera household has the joint kaimada of Karoona and Karanacchi. It can be observed in the rituals and practices of various communities of Kodagu that equal respect and love are shown to men and women.

The birth of a girl child is announced by striking a bronze plate. Whereas, gunshots are fired from a rifle to announce the birth of a boy child. Though it appears on the surface that this practice indicates discrimination between a girl and a boy, the reality has to be analysed in the background of the local culture.

The local culture has the tradition of young men joining the army by choice. Consequently, the birth of a baby boy implies the birth of a hero who will protect the country. Hence, the birth of a baby boy is announced through gunfire. This is corroborated by the information given by an elder. He said that before guns and gun powder were invented, a just-born baby boy was made to hold a bow and arrows made with the stalk of leaves. Bows, arrows, guns and gun powder are symbols of a valiant soldier. Similarly, the birth of a baby girl is announced by striking a bronze plate that is used to eat lunch. This symbolises the wish that the baby girl would grow into a woman who would feed everyone in the bronze plate like Goddess Annapurneshwari; she would  shoulder the responsibility of the entire family and take it to prosperity. The striking of the bronze plate is a unique way by which such a message is conveyed to the society. Before a marriage is fixed, the horoscope of a bride is kept a secret, and the horoscope of the groom is asked for by the family of the bride for matching (unlike in other communities).

During marriages, all communities conduct the ritual of 'filling the suitcase' of the bride. Parents keep in mind the necessities of their daughter and fill her suitcase with many things. The poor also do so, even by borrowing loans.  Elders have laid down this practice since they have the foresight that the bride's self-respect must be preserved.

The bride who enters the groom's house after marriage is provided with all her daily needs in her suitcase, from a small thing like a needle to other things such as the plate with which she eats, a bed, clothes, utensils, soap, and even some money. This is an unwritten law framed by elders so that the bride who is trying to adapt to a new home, family and ambience does not have to feel embarrassed asking for her needs. Such practices are in vogue even now.

When a married woman becomes a mother, she is taken care of very well, in terms of her physical and mental well-being. If the bride's parents are hard-pressed for money, the family of the groom extends financial help in the form of ethkarchu (childbirth allowance). The expenses of post-natal care of the woman must be borne by the family of the husband too.

Widow remarriage has social sanction among Kodavas. The custom of one of the brothers of the deceased husband remarrying the widow is also prevalent.

A folk song related to this issue, found in 'PattolePalame', says;

Chothchoth chunnaai thedigond pokane,
Thedipona paaballi kaalke thorebudda,
Ennanend ariviraa? Thaanda anna Devaiah kaalakandponalli,
Anna becha momma pandiyanadpole,
Ponnaainad koluendenninenethith,
Cheelanalla baalanbaipirinji bandit, Machimanek kerith
Thannapethaavva ngeesuddinaarpichi.

Failing repeatedly to find a much-needed medicinal creeper,
When one is returning disappointed,
The medicinal creeper that one went searching for
Entangles to one's feet.
Do you wonder how it can happen?
When a young man's elder brother Devayya
Departed responding to the call of Time,
He left behind attige*.
After knowing, thinking so and being aware
That according to the tradition of the elders
The young man can take her as his wife,
He is prepared to marry her.
He comes back to the house of his elders,
And gives the news to his mother.

*(attige – elder brother's wife)*

We come to know from this folk song that the Kodava society has a rich culture formed on a humane plane wherein a younger brother-in-law marries the widow of his elder brother and gives her a new life. It is to be noted that widow remarriage had the approval of elders and the society from times immemorial. Similarly, when a woman becomes a member of another family by way of marriage, the society ensures that she does not suffer because of any slighting of her honour and self-respect.

If a family does not have male children, but only daughters, one of the daughters is married to a groom who stays with the bride's family. He is made the inheritor according to the custom of kutti nippo (one who secures the lineage). This is done with the intention that the household should not come to an end. It is called okkaparije and kuttaparije.

Kodava folk culture has the unique feature of creating opportunities for rehabilitating women in distress. If a woman goes astray or becomes a widow, she is not abandoned - whichever be the class, sect or community she hails from. Instead, she is given a chance to live in the society again through such humanitarian measures as remarriage or widow remarriage.

Tribal communities such as Erava and Kuruba display high regard for women. The Eravas have matrilineal culture. After being married, a groom begins to live in the house of the bride. The Kurubas give a girl the freedom of marrying the young man she likes. If a girl elopes with a young man she likes and goes into the forest, the elders bring the two back and marry them as per tradition, in the presence of all.

The worship of Goddess Shakti (Female deity as the embodiment of energy) and Earth as a goddess is very common. The primordial mother of the clan is called Kanitayi. During Cauvery Sankramana (the annual resurgence of the river Cauvery), an idol of the Mother is made and kani worship is offered to it. El takeyakki tayi (the primordial mothers of the seven generations of a lineage) and kodachi taayi (martyrs) are worshipped. Usually, every village has the shrine of Bhagavathi, a form of Goddess Shakti. The people worship Bhadrakaali, Chamundi,

Bhagavathi, Karingaali, Kaveramma, Parvathi, Mandatavve, Dabbacchavve, Maaramma, Pannangaanthamma and other female deities with great fervour and devotion.

It is also to be noted that the society which, on the one hand, has a strong humanitarian base in matters such as women's freedom and equality has, on the other, imposed restrictions on women. This can be seen in its folklore. For example, there is no provision for traditionally sanctioned celebration at the time of a woman's remarriage. It is performed in a simple way in the form of koodavali (coming together). Whereas, there are no such restrictions for a man each time he marries. He has the freedom of marrying seven times. But, in the case of the marriage of a daughter, the elders worry about the expenses that have to be incurred.[Please let me know if this practice is prevalent even now. If not, these lines have to be changed to past tense]

A widow is not entitled to any form of decoration. She cannot use vermilion, flowers, colour dresses, ornaments or cosmetics. She has to wear only a pure white saree. During the funeral of the husband, the vermilion on the forehead of the wife is erased, her mangalasutra (an auspicious symbol married women wear) is snatched and the glass bangles she wears on her hands are broken. This obnoxious practice is still in vogue in this society.

It would not be wrong to say that the social and political circumstances of the past were responsible for elders to impose such restrictions on widows. The women of this region are beautiful, naturally endowed with an attractive physique. If such women decorate themselves, they attract the attention of lustful men. We come to know from the history of this region that some of the kings who ruled here were womanisers. It is quite possible that the elders imposed some restrictions on widows in order to protect them from such lecherous persons.

Similarly, some of the proverbs in the folklore mention the problems faced by parents who give birth to daughters:

A field where monkeys are abundant and a house in which there are more girls will not prosper. (kodaperthamakkiyuponnperthamaneyuuaaga)

Or, a field in which monkeys are in abundance and a mother who gives birth to more number of daughters will not prosper.

Elders composed this proverb from their experience of observing families where there were a number of girls, or mothers who gave birth to a number of daughters.

This is so because a girl's parents should incur expenses towards her marriage, post-delivery care and the naming ceremony of the baby. Even after a girl is married, her natal house (parents' family) has some responsibilities towards her. Keeping these issues in mind, the elders composed the above –mentioned proverbs out of their experience.

Similarly, there is a rule in the society that a woman should not touch a plough. This matter can be analysed as follows:

It is said, "The one who tills a piece of land is its owner". But, statements such as , "A woman who tills a piece of land is its owner" or "Those who till a piece of land are its owners" are not in vogue among the common people. In the local folk culture, an elderly person of a family named pattedaara plays the most prominent role in matters related to land. The approval and signature of the pattedara carry tremendous significance when land is transferred. But, the wife of the elderly person who is recognised as the pattedaara in the family has no right or importance in such matters. Whereas, the wife of a prominent person of the family called koravukaara is given the status of koravukarti, and shown respect. These facts make it clear that the society which has disallowed women from touching a plough has no qualms in using them abundantly for work in the farm, and it reveals the selfishness of the patriarchal society which wants only men to be owners of land.

A man keeps his foot wherever he sees slushSimilarly, he washes himself wherever he sees water. (Aankethekandallichoutu, neerkandallikathu)

The above proverb seems to justify the illegitimate actions of a man. But, if a woman goes astray, she is called as "The one who is like a defiled pot (A pot defiled by a dog)" and she is viewed with severe contempt. Another proverb says, "The voice of women should not even reach the ceiling of the house". This makes it clear that a woman's freedom of speech is restricted to the house.

It is true that motherhood plays a crucial role in determining a woman's stature. But, there were some instances when it was taken to an extreme. Folklore has evidence of such instances.  The ritual paitandek alpa felicitated a woman who gave birth to ten children as 'Mahataayi' (a great mother), but it ddid not seem to have cared for the woman's health and the condition of her body. This is because the continuation of the family lineage was given more importance, and there was no concern for the woman's health.

The following proverb introduces the social system that looked down upon an 'infertile' woman:

You are very beautiful to look at,

O Booraga flower! But nobody

Decorates their hair with you since you lack fragrance. (kaambakknalloremurkrapoov , naarathangallachoodathaninna)

<hr>

Since the booraga flower does not give out any fragrance, it is not worn on the hair as an embellishment, or used in worship, though it is beautiful. Similarly, a married woman who does not beget a child is not shown respect, love and regard in the society.

Giving birth to a child and becoming a mother are not the social responsibilities of a woman. It is not justified to make her the target of condemnation for not having children. Besides, it is inhuman that, holding the wife responsible for not having a child, a husband marries another woman while the wife is still alive. This practice produces greater mental agony to one who is already in sorrow that she does not have a child. It amounts to her own family harassing her instead of sympathising with her agony.

Every year, a ritual named beduhabba(b0dnamme) is performed for different deities in all temples across Kodagu. During this cultural event, men dress up as women and perform a dance called soolekali as a form of offering thanks to god for favours received. Similarly, a traditional dance named kundanchoole is performed during the village festival of Maggula village. A thanks-giving ritual named pommangala is performed in the temple of Baadagarakeri wherein boys are dressed up as girls.

Some of the cultural practices mentioned above indicate the honour that women are accorded in the folk culture of Kodagu. This is the way by which god is pleased by men who disguise themselves as women.

It is to be noted that many communities impose disgusting restrictions on women such as the dowry system, regulations that they should not move around in the presence of men, the wife must eat only in the plate left behind by the husband after he has eaten, and her life is confined to the kitchen. It is worth observing that such disgusting restrictions imposed on women are not seen in the folk culture of Kodagu.

In sum, the culture of the society in Kodagu has given love, equality, freedom of expression and encouragement to women and thereby developed unique cultural practices. These features have been expressed in its folklore in a unique and impressive manner.

**Bibliography**


Nadakeriyanda Chinnappa, Pattole Palame

Nagaraj M.G, The Haleri Dynasty

Ramanujam P.S., Kodavas


**Resource Persons:**

KaravatteeraAyyanna
1. MukkaateeraAyyappa
2. Kolera Ponnappa (Virajapete taluk, Kodagu district)

# Tradition of Aiyyappa God in Kodagu Culture

*Dr. Lalitha K. P.*

With the decline of the Roman empire, the spice trade with the Kerala coast was taken over by the Arabs, long before the advent of Islam itself. Precisely when Islam came to Kerala is not definitively known. But the Arabic tradition suggests, that there could be a possibility they might have entered Kerala when a few missionaries were sent out by the Prophet in his fifty-seventh year. If this is true, Islam might have entered Kerala in the seventh century Itself. According to Sheikh Zainuddin, the 16th-century historian who visited Kerala, an important missionary group consisting of Malik Ibn Dinar, SharafIbn Malik, Malik IbnHabib, and others landed in Cranganore (Kannanur) in 642- 643 A.D. and were warmly received by the ruler. The group divided itself into two, both moving along the coast, one northwards and the other towards the south. The tolerance of the native rulers enabled them to establish eleven centers during the first phase. Around the Mosques which began to be constructed, colonies of Muslims grew up and owing to the continuance of the mercantile tradition of the Arabs, these colonies became important commercial centers linking the west coast with West Asia and North Africa.

We have now to move on to a fascinating Hindu religious tradition that established a fine contact with Islam amidst the vicissitude of medieval history. This tradition is that of Sastha or Ayyappa. Originally, Ayyan or Ayyappan seems to have been the protective deity of Dravidian villages, on either side of the ghats, that is in Tamil country as well as in Kerala. Village shrines showing the deity mounted on a charger and armed with bows and arrows can be seen even today in Tamil country, where, however, the evolution seems to have been arrested at this level. As Kerala was mainly occupied by the migrant groups from the east coast through the mountain passes, and as the first settlements were made by clearing the thick forests, the deity of the village became the deity of the forest. This recalls the growth of a myth in the Greco-Roman world, where 'Pan' was the protective deity of Arcadian shepherds and the Arcadian forests and later emerged 'Faunus', the god of agricultural communities in ancient Italy. Ayyappan thus became a forester, his hunting pack consisted of tigers, not dogs, and his most ancient and important shrine is in the forested Sabri hill on the spine of the ghats overlooking the central plain of both Tamil country and Kerala.

When Buddhism spread to Kerala, Ayyappan seems to have been worshipped as the Buddha. The fact that the worship of Ayyappan, throughout the ages, tolerated no caste distinctions and that even today the pilgrims to his forest - shrine chant the salutation 'Ayyappansaranam', reminding us of the 'SaranaTraya' of the Buddhist orders, this phase helps us recall the growth of the myth. When the Saivite religion displaced Buddhism, the folk imagination regarded him as the son of Siva, When rivalry developed between the Saivite and the Vaishnavite cults, Ayyappan again become a reconciler. There exists a fantastic legendaccording to which Vishnu once took a female form, and Siva became enamored by her and the fruit of the union was Ayyappan.

The next phase brings us to a historical figure. The second Cheraempire collapsed in the conflict with Cholas in the eleventh century. The realm disintegrated into small principalities, none of which were strong enough to arrest the growing anarchy. From across the Ghats, the Pandyan rulers began to encroach into Kerala and claim lordship over the principalities. The Maravas, who were lawless tribes of the ancient Dravidian realm, lived by plunder like the Vikings of

Europe, they occupied the forested spines of the Ghats and frequently raided the plains of central Kerala. The west coast similarly, saw the frequent visits from Arab pirates.

Pantalam was a small principality in central Kerala. In one of the raids by the Maravas, a princess disappeared and was believed to have perished. But she had been rescued by a Brahmin youth. They fled to a forest retreat near the Sabari hill. In course of time, a son was born to them. The father brought up the boy in both an intense spiritual and military discipline, the latter because he wanted his son to rescue Kerala from anarchy. When he came of age, the youth was sent to the court of Pantalam where the ruler recognized him as the son of his long - lost sister and made him the commander of his army. Ayyappan, as the youth was called, later visited all the principalities of Kerala, mobilizing their support for a united onslaught against the Maravas and establishing Kalaris (military gymnasia) all over the land.

A remarkable encounter with the Arab pirates resulted in a great friendship between Ayyappan and their leader, Vavar (Babur). Today Vavar's shrine stands near Ayyappan's temple on Sabari hill and not only Muslims but Hindu pilgrims also offer worship here. From the family which traces its descent from Vavar, the eldest in every generation participate in the annual festival of the Sabari hill temple, and 'Vavar Swami' is revered as a saint by the Hindu pilgrims. The syncretic vitality of the Ayyappan myth, thus, could unite not only the different cults of Hinduism but the different religions as well. Ayyappan later visited the Pandyan court to ensure that when he finally moved against the Maravas, the Pandyan ruler would stand in support of him and not the Maravas. This was necessary because the Maravas were, nominally at least, the subjects of the Pandyan king and provided recruits for his army, although the bulk of them were freebooters who ignored his authority. The rest of the story deals with the brilliant military operations against Marava strongholds in the hills where Vavar was one of Ayyappan's most trusted lieutenants. After the campaign, the temple which had been destroyed decades ago was restored and according to the legend, Ayyappan himself mysteriously disappeared, as his mission was over.

Today the figure of this national hero of the eleventh or twelfth century has indissolubly merged with that of the traditional deity. The Ayyappan cult has had phenomenal growth in recent years which deserves a detailed sociological study. The annual pilgrimage to the forest - shrine attracts increasing numbers every year, and from the educated classes. Probably, the entire experience is felt to be a vigorous toning up of the otherwise routine life in civic occupations. Before the pilgrimage, for thirty days the devotee has to adopt a strict regimen of physical and mental cleanliness. Neither caste nor class barriers are tolerated among the pilgrims who address one another as "Ayyappa Swami' (Lord Ayyappa). It is this intense democratic spirit that enables the cult to link up smoothly with the Islamic tradition as well.

Village-deities are an All - India phenomenon. By this, it means that the deities who are worshiped in villages in various parts of India have more or less the same character and attributes and that the technique of propitiating them is broadly similar. These statements no doubt sound vague and general, but any attempt to make them more precise will have to take account of exceptions at every point.

While the phenomenon is broadly similar all over India, there are important regional variations. Generally speaking, within India, each region or district has a greater unity than the larger area of which it is a part. Inside peninsular India, for instance, each linguistic area represents an area of greater cultural homogeneity and social solidarity- But there are cultural forms which are common to two or more linguistic areas. Malayalam and Tamil areas have certain cultural forms in common; and similarly, Kannada, Telugu, and Marathi areas have some cultural forms in common. Within each linguistic area, there are differences of their own; cultural forms present in the center of a linguistic area might not be present in the peripheral regions or present only in an altered form. Geographical barriers also usually represent Cultural barriers. For instance, cultural forms found in the littoral stripe have great difficulty in spreading into the mainland of peninsular India. A country like Kodagu, which lies at the periphery of three linguistic areas, Karmada, Malayalam, and Tulu, has certain cultural forms in common with each of them, and it is mainly due to regular contact and diffusion of cultural elements.

Throughout south India village - deities are represented by crude images of stone or wood. They are either housed in shrines which are usually not very elaborate or simply embedded in the earth without a roof above them. In Kodagu an Ayyappa deity dedicated to a keri [hamlet] is frequently found either at the foot of a tree or in the shade of a grove on a raised earthen platform with a pack of earthen hunting dogs. This cult might have entered Kodagu in the 12th century A.D. from Kerala. In Kodagu, Shasta is referred to as Ayyappa or Saasthaavu, and he inhabits the forest in which he wanders at night with his favorite pack of dogs. At night, in the forest, he can be heard whistling to his pack. Votive offerings of representations of dogs and bows and arrows are made to his shrines. Some forests are reserved for Ayyappa exclusively, and nobody may hunt or cut down trees there. Kodavas do not hunt on Wednesdays and Saturdays because Ayyappa hunts on those days. Formerly, liquor and fowl were offered to him by Kodavas after a successful hunt. At some Ayyappa shrines, non-vegetarian offerings are made, whereas at others only vegetarian offerings are made.

Kodavas are fond of hunting, and every ancestral house has a pack of dogs that accompany their master during hunting. Ayyappa is extremely popular with Kodavas as the deity presiding overhunting, and many Kodavas are named after him. The forests reserved on the name of Ayyappa are called as Deverakaadu. Worship may or may not be offered daily at these shrines. There is no uniform rule applicable in this matter. Practices vary from village to village, and in some temples, worship is offered once a week, while others come to life only annually, or once every few years, when the festival of the deity is being celebrated.

**Bibliography**


1.  Mysore and Coorg. Vol. III - Coorg. Editor - Benjamin Lewis Rice

2.  Gazetteer of Coorg. - G. Richter

3.  A study of the Origins of Coorgs by Lt. Col. K.C. Ponnappa - 1997.

4.  The Coorgs and their Origins by M.P. Cariappa and PonnammaCariappa - 1981.

5.  Kodavas and their Gala and Lela - by I.M. Muthanna - 1987.

6.  Archaeology of Coorg by Dr. K.K. Subbayya - 1978.

7.  Caste and Tribes of South India - Edgar Thurston - 1909.

8.  Religion and Society among the Coorgs of South India - by M.N. Srinivas - 1951.

# An Analysis of SACRED GROVES with Special Reference to Coorg

*Dr. Lalitha K. P.*

## ABSTRACT

This document gives an Analysis of the Sacred Grooves (Devara Kaadu) in Coorg (Kodagu), a district in Karnataka state, India. In this paper, an attempt has been made to discuss various aspects of Sacred Grooves in Coorg as presented. An analysis of Social and Environmental concerns of people in Coorg has been done with an emphasis on the unique concept of Devara Kaadu in Kodagu.

**Keywords:** Coorg, Kodagu, Sacred Grooves, Devarara Kaadu.

## INTRODUCTION

In every society on this planet, there is a sharp distinction between the holy, the ordinary, and the unholy. 'The sacred' are the things set apart by a peculiar emotional attitude, usually of respect and awe. They are imbued with special powers either advantageous or dangerous. They are not to be used in an everyday utilitarian context, but are reserved for special occasions and hedged about with taboos and restrictions of all sorts.

The important question in the study of 'Devara Kaadu' or 'Sacred Forests or Groves' therefore becomes 'What is the source of the sacred'? The question is baffling but not incapable of a solution. The sacred thing here is something tangible – a physical object such as a plant, a flag, a color, a word, a place, an act, the sun, the moon, the wind, the fire, the water, and whatnot. Hence the observer has too frequently tried to derive the sacred from these objects themselves.

To some cow is sacred, to some a tree is sacred, to some fire is sacred, to some sun is sacred, and to some all-natural things are sacred. So the sacredness deals with the object which a particular group worships. So there is cow worshiping religion, tree worshiping religion, sun worshiping religion, fire worshiping religion, etc.

## SACRED GROVES – CONCEPT AND ORIGIN

Since the dawn of civilization or the advent of Homo sapiens, different forms of worship have evolved. The objects of worship differ from place to place, but the main underlying principle of worship has been propitiating to Nature and Environment. The early man has always held Nature in awe as he realized that he has to depend on Nature for his basic needs such as- air, water, food, and light; perhaps, that is why, the early man held Nature at a position of great respect, fierce devotion and started worshiping Nature as God – the powerful and the giver. An aura of sacredness thus started towards all the elements in Nature which are easily perceptible such as the Forests, Rivers, Trees, Mountains, Sun, and Moon, etc.

As the people grew in numbers so did their hunger for basic needs and their attitudes; along with the desire for food, the desire for other carnal necessities grew which they tried satisfying from the very surroundings that they held sacred. This led to indiscriminate tapping of Nature.

Sacred Groves existed in different parts of the world such as in South America, Africa, Australia, Greece, and Rome, even in France, Germany, and in almost all parts of Asia. The concept of Sacred Groves was not limited to any particular place or race of a community.

In Indian culture, there is a special identity and religiosity given to the trees, animals, plants, birds, and even insects. Sacred Groves and its habitant can be found in all regions. SARANE in Bengal and Bihar, VARAN in Rajasthan, DEVARI in Maharashtra, KAAVU in Kerala and Tamilnadu are specially identified places held in great esteem and revered as such even now.

It is estimated in India the Sacred Groves extended to about 39,063 hectares consisting of about 4125 Groves approximately. In Karnataka, all districts have forest covers earmarked as Devara-Kaadu and have local names such as 'KAN' in Uttara Kannada district, 'NAGABANA' in Dakshina Kannada, 'GRAMA DEVATA' Forest Hassan district. Cattle wealth is held sacred in all places and 'GOMALAS'- grazing field for cattle exclusively is a distinct feature in all towns and villages.

In Kodagu, according to some legendary perception, 'KADAMBA TREE' (Anthocephanecadamba) associated with Chandravarma is considered as the progenitor of Kodavas who belonged to Kadamba dynasty, It has been held sacred and worshiped; thus the early indigenous race of Kodagu were worshipers of their ancestors and Nature and in memory of these, 'Devarakaadus' were nurtured in every village. Each village has its meadows, a Temple, an Ambala, and every household a Kaimada a memorial for the ancestor. The ancestors realized the importance of Forest wealth and to preserve the wealth and to see that the succeeding generations do not exploit this to satisfy their greed, an aura of fierce discipline and devotion with religiosity symbols were created. Certain festivities and ceremonies were held in such areas with religious fervor, devotion and cooperation are being continued even now. Such practices have helped in preserving the Devara- Kaadus in Kodagu to a substantial extent compared to being less prevalent in other parts of the world.

---

# UNIQUENESS OF 'DEAVARA KAADUS' OF KODAGU

Sacred Groves or sanctified sanctuary or 'Devarakaadu' in local parleys can be found in many parts of the world over and indeed in every state in India. Over time due to degradation as a result of improper attention, such sanctuaries are fast disappearing. Devarakaadus in Kodagu has still retained some of its flavor and distinct characteristics. It stands quite apart from the rest of the Devarakaadus elsewhere.

a.  As per Forest Department's statistics, there are about 1214 Devarakaadus with coverage of 2500 hectares in Kodagu district; nowhere else can one find in such large numbers and in terms of area. The total coverage is about 2 percent of the district. It is claimed as a world record.

b.  In terms of density, there is one Devarakaadu for every 300 very rare acres.

c.  In 20 villages of the district, each village has ten Devarakaadus.

d.  All indigenous communities unique in their way take part in every ritual, festival, etc. conducted in Devarakaadu displaying harmony and camaraderie.

e.  The tribes and aborigines have identified more than 100 deities with Devarakaadus of their area of concern; this is also a world record.

f.  Each Devarakaadu has its unique type of celebrations like folk games, folk arts, dances, songs, rituals as appropriate to the deities associated with the kaadu.

g.  Every Devarakaadu is full of rarest trace species of life forms and living creatures like birds, beetles, fowls, herbs, and animals giving it a distinct flavor special to each kaadu.

The vastness of DevaraKaadu I Kodagu is illustrated by the following details available in Forest Department Records:

| Taluk | Numbers | Acres |
| --- | --- | --- |
| Virajpet | 508 | 2,180 |
| Somavarpet | 400 | 2,860 |
| Madikere | 306 | 1,335 |
| Total | 1214 | 6,375 |

The quantity of Devarakaadus is quite large for a small district like Kodagu as compared to any such similar areas elsewhere in the world.

As per Forest Department records, the five major Devarakaadus in Kodagu districts are –

1. PaadiIgguthappaDevarakaadu of Kunjila village-358 acres.
2. EshwaraAppandriappaDevarakaadu of Katakeri village-323 acres.
3. BasaveshwaraDevarakaadu of Valnur-Thyagathur village-304 acres.
4. MahavishnuDevarakaadu of Kopati village-208 acres.
5. AiyappaDevarakaadu of Madae village-141 acres.

The actual area of big farms needs to be updated. In Thakeri village of Somavarpet taluk, a maximum of 17 Devarakaadus can be found. In about 39 villages there are more than 7 kaadus per each village. Maximum numbers can be found in Valnur, Keerkodali, and Haleri.

In Virajpet taluk, maximum number of Devarakaadus can be found in Kuttaandi, Mythaadi, Hudikeri, Maggula, Bilagunda and Deavanageri villages.

In Madikeri taluk, the maximum numbers of Devarakaadus can be found in Maragod, Kolakeri, Biligiri, Hosakeri, Madae, and Kirundad villages.

The reason why the number varies in large numbers in each village is perhaps the earlier single integrated kaadus must have been divided into smaller eco units associated with local communities and their Deities.

## VARIETY, DIVERSITY, AND CLASSIFICATION

Dr. Chandrakant and Sri M.G. Nagaraj have in their study of 'Devarakaadus of Kodagu' have arrived at some classifications according to certain characteristics inherent in various regions –

1   Basadis or Jina Forests – Temple properties. References are found in Archives in Madikeri and Mullure inscriptions.

2   Paisari Forests – These are controlled by Forest Department; however, maintained and protected by the local communities.

3   Holae Devarakaadu – Certain caste called Kembattis are guarding this and holdings identified with a variety of deities,  among them female deity Pannangalathammae, Chaundi, Ayyappa are important.

4   Kaimadakaad or Kaaronakaad – Mausoleums are built (a pyramid-like structure) in memory of the founder ancestor whom the Kodava call Karona and flora are developed around these structures. Such areas are found in many holdings of Kodava families.

5   Suggikaad (Suggibana) – Certain trees or plants developed as mini forests and dedicated to certain deities as per local indigenous practices. The

majority of these can be found in Somavarpet taluk. Dailypoojas are performed to Goddess Parvathi and Saptamatha. Along with that, we can find Heddevarabana, Gramadevathabana, and Beeredevarabana.

6    Certain forest areas are donated to various Matts by the erstwhile Rajas of Kodagu; mostly confined to Virajpet and Somavarpettaluks.

7    Certain clans called 'Jamma Mapilae' (converted ethnic race) are maintaining certain areas of forest land within their entitled holdings. These are called 'Pallikaad' and can be found in Srimangala, Ponnampet, Mythaadi, Chamiyala, and in some other places.

8    'Poo Kaad' (Flower Grove) – Many a type of flower-bearing trees grown since the 14th Century A.D., dedicated to the deity 'Poovistana' (God of flowers) can be found in temple towns of Bhagamandala, Paalur, and other places.

9    Beerabana (Veeravana) – Groves dedicated to great warriors (in their names); again these are confined to certain families who have produced many warriors of repute.

The above-mentioned classification illustrates the uniqueness of various types of Devarakaadus of Kodagu which is maintained by each family (Okka): village, the local bodies, or communion of people as a part of their inherent culture integrated with Nature.

## DEITIES ASSOCIATED WITH VARIOUS DEVARA KAADUS

In the three principal taluks (Virajpet, Somavarpet, and Madikeri), Deities identified and method of worship, festivals vary in each region something peculiar areas of each place-often influenced by the neighboring border areas and the practices followed there.

Thus the Devarakaadus around Virajpet taluk is mostly influenced by bordering Kerala. Names of Lord Ayyappa, Goddess Bhagavati, Bhadrakaali are common and in a majority; in addition to local names of MahadevaBasaveswara, Durga and Maramma. The temple and other buildings' architecture styles resemble those of Kerala style. The worshiping practice is also imitative of Kerala. Village Oracle (man possessed by spirit) speaks in the Malayalam language.

In Madikeri taluk, the mixed influence of Kerala and adjoining Dakshina Kannada is seen. Names like Sampaje, Thodikana, Baathrae, Nagabana, Panjuruli, Korthi, Shastha are very common.

In Somavarpet taluk – similarly, the names and practices are influenced by the bordering plain areas like Hassan and Mysore. Worshiping of Eshwara and Parvathi and its local forms like Subbamma, Kenchamma, Kunthyamma, etc is thus the practice. In these areas the village or family head if chieftain is addressed as chief instead of 'Thakka' as found in Virajpet and Madikeri taluks. The folk arts, songs, festivals, etc also bear resemblance to the respective neighboring influences.

The Devarakaadus of Kodagu, harbors various types of flora and fauna, that exist from time immemorial. These play a vital role seemingly and unseemingly in our lives. Certain life forms that exist in Kodagu are quite distinctive and particular to this region not found anywhere else in the country. Wildlife experts from the Oxford forest organization after conducting extensive studies for well over three years have expressed the opinion that though Devarakaadus occupy a small percentage of the land area it has about 45 percent of various species plants, 36 percent of various birds and 18 percent of other species of fungi, etc. Though wildlife of the kind of Elephants and Tigers are found very rarely in Devarakaadus, their smaller cousins are surviving in large numbers. With the advent of coffee estates, this kind of native trees and animals are confined only in smaller areas like Devarakaadus. Trees like silver oak, Mangium are found around these estates and the other local varieties are dwindling along with the life form which it supports. The future generation will never be able to see these in course of time if Devarakaadus are not properly preserved. Sanctuaries like Nagaraholae, Brahmagiri forests, Puspagiri forests, and Bio farms around Talakavery are protected and preserved through government support and other agencies. But this is not sufficient. The 1214 numbers of Devarakaadus in villages should be looked after properly with support from all concerned.

Economic aspects – The plants grown in Devarakaadus have great medicinal values both for humans and animals. Highly valuable trees like Devadar, Beeti, Agini, Jack fruit trees are felled after their life period and are given to Forest Department and Temple trusts. They are used for structures, furniture, etc. Many creepers, ferns, cane are useful in many ways in our life. Many fruits also have nutritional and medicinal values. By and large the forest cover itself serves as a storage reservoir and buffer of water recycling as it is capable of sustaining any amount of rain-absorbing and recycling.

Now the ecology of Kodagu has completely changed. How different Kodagu would have been having our grandfathers been alive today! If we had them at the forefront of the environment movement, they would then have prevailed upon us to set an example if simple, ecologically sound living for the benefit of all people. Our forefathers were environment prophets whose precious lives were reserved to safeguard the ecological balance on the earth.

There are many reasons for the disappearance of Devarakaadus. Many Devarakaadus have been encroached by migrants from the outside district, coffee cultivators, land grabbers and some have been converted into small village units by some communities. These have been done right under the nose of the very guardians of the Devarakaadus. The timber has been used for providing shelter to the socially and economically deprived. The indifference of local people, family and village heads, forest department officials, government, and panchayats have added to the woes of the Devarakaadu. Lack of coordination between the revenue officials and forest officials and their callous attitude is another factor. Some vested interests have taken political mileage out of the large influx of migrant laborers of coffee estates and the like. Post-1888, Devarakaadus have been given the status as protected forest and declared as belonging to the department; thus no single family can claim absolute right over these forests. (Probably at best they can maintain them as free leaseholds). Despite this, no action is being taken on the land grabbers. Many protected forests have been misused, abused, and worst vandalized. The entire ecosystem has almost disappeared. Devarakaadus have gradually lost their pristine purity and glory. Rare species of plants, creatures, and other life forms have disappeared. Even the festivities associated with certain Devarakaadus have lost their importance and veneration once practiced as a community of yore. The government and locals should.....................................save the forests.

## THE [hidden] WEALTH AND BENEFITS OF DEVARA KAADU'S TREASURE

Bio Treasure – Many of the domestic and commercial crops like pepper, cardamom, turmeric, ginger, root – vegetables like sweet potato, arum colocasia, yam, etc had their origin in forests of yesteryears. To find out remedies to get rid of the usual diseases that affect these crops, one has to find out from the plants of the forest the 'Genes' required. The infamous 'Wilt' disease can be removed by researching into the forest varieties. Through extensive research in Bio-Tech have various patents can be made and rights sold. It is believed that not so long ago a certain disease that affected paddy crop was got rid of using a good breed from a wild sanctuary in Kerala.

## CONCLUSION

In Devarakaadus of Kodagu various types of Ferns, Fungi, and tree moss are found unique to the region. These are very valuable for processing various types of herbal medicines. These forms of species are needed for maintaining eco-balance in the plant kingdom. Certain types of mushroom Xylaria, Ganoderma has been found in many Devarakaadus. There is a lot of demand for these in the world market. Gainful use can be made of by the preservation of forest for further propagation of these life forms.

# REFERENCES


| 1 | A History of Kodagu | 2012 | P.S. Appaiah |
| 2 | A Mannual of Coorg - A Gazetteer | 1870 | Richter G. Delhi |
| 3 | Archaeology of Coorg, | 1978 | Subbaiah K.K. Mysore |
| 4 | A Study of the origins of Coorgs | 1997 | K.C. Ponnappa |
| 5 | Coorg Memoirs | 1855 | Moogling H. Bangalore |
| 6 | Coorg and the Coorgs | 1931 | Muthanna Pandanda |
| 7 | Coorg District Gazetteer | 1965 (Ed) | B.N. Satyan, Bangalore |
| 8 | Coorg Land of Beauty and Valour | 2010 | P.T. Bopanna |
| 9 | Dateline Coorg | 200 | P.T. Bopanna Rolling Stone Publications, Bangalore |
| 10 | Discover Coorg | 2008 | P. T. Bopanna Prism Books Pvt. Ltd. Bangalore |
| 11 | Epigraphia Carnatica | 1914 (Ed) | Rice Edn. Revised, Vol. I Coorg District |
| 12 | Epigraphia Carnatica | 1905 | B.L. Rice, Vol. IX |
| 13 | Ethnographical compendiumon the castes and Tribes found in the province of Coorg. | 1887 | Richter G. Bangalore |
| 14 | Ganapathy B.D. | 1980 | Kodavas, Madikeri |
| 15 | Indian Chronological Tables | 1977 | (Ed) Dr. B.S. Kulakarni, Karnataka University |
| 16 | Kodavas | 1980 | B.D. Ganapathy, Jyothi Prakashana, Temple Road, Madikeri |


---

# Tippu Sultan – In the eyes of people of Coorg

*Dr. Lalitha K. P.*

## ABSTRACT

This document gives an Analysis of life of Tippu Sultan in the perspective of people of Coorg (Kodagu), a district in Karnataka state, India on the basis of History of Coorg. In this paper an attempt has been made to discuss various aspects of life of people in Coorg as seen in the pages of history during the time of Tippu Sultan. An analysis of Social and Political Life of people in Coorg has been done with an emphasis on caste system, tribal life and religious beliefs of people during this time to throw light on the personality of Tippu Sultan especially in the matter of Forcible Religious Conversion.

**Keywords:** Coorg, Kodagu, Kodava, Forcible Conversion.

## INTRODUCTION

Among the kings of India who opposed the suzerainty of the British, Tippu Sultan of Mysore occupies the prime place. He assumes an important position not only in the history of Mysore but also in the history of India as brilliant general, a matured administrator, shrewd politician and a man of virtues.

## DETAIL AND DISCUSSION

The rise of Tippu Sultan is a critical phase in the history of modern India. The British had just begun their efforts to establish their hegemony over India. Sensing the political intensity Tippu was convinced that the British were his staunch enemies and hence did all efforts to thwart their plans. He waged three wars against them and finally was killed while trying to retain his independence. He is a winger person in the history who died in battle field while fighting the enemies.  His valor, war strategy and leadership qualities were appreciated by the European generals which speak of his greatness as a ruler.

However, such a vibrant picture of Tippu's personality cannot be seen as for as Coorg history is concerned. The reason being Tippu had inflicted serious wounds in the minds of the people of Coorg.  Though he has been depicted in the history of India as either a tragic hero or a hero, he is a villain as far as coorg history is concerned.  That is precisely because in the eyes of the people of Coorg Tippu is cruel, criminal, selfish and an opportunist.

This contradiction in his personality has led to confusion among historians. The purpose of this write up is to record some of my observations about Tippu's dual personality.

There is absolutely no difference of opinion regarding Tippu as a great administrator and a fighter.  But whether he was a communal or a blind follower of Islam is a question which haunts everyone when we deal with the history of Coorg. Therefore, it is apt here to turn our attention towards the opinions expressed by some of historians and intellectuals.

Western writers like Edward Thomas and G.T. Garret in their writings have complimented Tippu for his gallantry, administrative skill and zeal for reformation, interest for innovative ideas, scientific and clinical approach in dealing with the problems. According to historians like Dr. Shiek Ali and Kabir Kauser Tippu respected all religions and never indulged in    forced conversion.  This opinion has been endorsed by litterateurs' ties like Girish Karnad and H.S. Shivaprakash.

In support of their argument, these writers cite the examples of the grants made by Tippu Sultan to Sringeri Math, gifts given to Sri Ranganathswamy Temple at Srirangapatna and non-muslim officers holding high positions in Tippus's army.

Keeping aside this view of Tippu, it is imperative to draw our attention towards the following issues while picturing Tippu's personality from the perspective of the people of Coorg. Those who argue Tippu as a communal who indulged in forcible conversion of Hindus to Islam and also his love for 'Jihad' narrate the following view in support of their argument:

On careful examination of the Indian history, Tippu may be compared with Aurangazeb who was a religious bigot. During his 17 years of rule Tippu caused irrepairable damage to Hindu temples and also converted Hindus to Islam much against their wish. If Tippu were a religious tolerant why did he damage Hindu temples? Why did he indulge in forcible conversion? And why did he call the non muslims as kafirs in confidential letters?

In one such letter written on January 19, 1790 to one of his accomplices Badruz Juman Khan he writes: "Do you know about my recent victory in Malabar? I have converted over 4 lakh Kafirs to Islams. Now I have decided to fight against the cursed Raman Nair. I just want to convert him and his entire population to Islam".

It is this approach of Tippu that led to his downfall. Raja Raman Nair not only puts up a brave fight but also seeks the support of the British which resulted in the III Anglo-Mysore war. Lord Cornwallis allied with Dharmaraja of Tiruvankur. Further, with the alliance of Maratha and Nizam of Hyderabad Cornwallis invaded Mysore province from different directions. As a result, Tippu was forced to leave

Bangalore and retreat to the fort of Srirangapatna. Ultimately he had to surrender in 1792.

In order to avenge his defeat and get back those provinces which he had lost, he had to win the sympathy of local Hindus. We cannot rule out the fact that Tippu made grants to Sringeri math during this time. Several writers have analysed the letters written by Tippu.

Leela Prasad in his book, "Poetics of conduct: oral narrative and moral being in a south Indian town" and Surendra Nath Sen have expressed their opinion in the following manner: "The time when Tippu made grants to Sringeri Math during 1793 was very critical as he was hunted by his enemies. It became inevitable for him to regain the confidence of Hindu subjects at least temporarily. On the other hand, he also enticed the Marathas towards superstitious beliefs by performing homa and other rituals by Hindu priests and thereby caused fear among them."

To support his argument, we need to look at Tippu's belief in astrology. There were many astrologers in his court and Tippu used to fix proper muhurth for wars and invasions: V.R. Parameshwaran Pillai records such a belief in the following words. "Tippu had lot of faith in astrology. After the humiliating defeat in 1782, the astrologers of Tippu had predicted that he would become Badshah of South India, if he defeated the British. On their advice, Tippu started making gifts to Math and other temples. These gifts were made not out of his love and honour for Hindus, but with an eye to become the Badshah".

As far as Coorg is concerned we get certain instances where in Tippu dealt cruelly with the people of Coorg. Even today we can find the remnants of the Hindu temple which were destroyed by his army at Mavukal hills near Thithimathi. Similarly, there are many temples which have been ransacked by Tippu. The Jamma Mapilla community is still flourishing in Coorg which is evident to his forcible conversion.

During the 3rd Anglo-Mysore war, Tippu captured thousands of people from Kodagu and converted them to Islam in Srirangapatna. Some among them escaped and returned to their native places. Veera Rajendra of Coorg helped such people by giving them small pieces of dry land. The number of such people was about twelve thousand according to 'Rajendra Name'. Those who returned after conversion were supported by Mapillas of Malabar. Though originally they belong to Kodava Community they came to be recognized as Jamma Mapillas following Tippu's invasion. This community is found even today in places, Nalvathokkalu, Beguru, Chenivada, Mythadi, Kottoli and Kolakeri.

There are many instances to show that these Jamma Mapillas were basically Kodavas. They also have 'Inmane' like the Kodavas. Also they use cultural symbols like Dudi (tabala), weapons like Odikatthi and Piche Katthi. Similary, they also have family names like other Kodava communities. For example: Jamma Mapillas belonging to 'Alira' family are found in Beguru village near Ponnampet.

They also have Pallikad (protected forest) like 'Devkad' of other Kodava Communities. Palli happens to be their place of worship. However, they are declining their Kodava antecedent. Instead, they are tracing their links to Kerala. Hence the Mapillas are in a state of fix as they can neither claim as Hindu nor admit themselves as Muslims. Tippu Sultan is responsible for this kind of predicament.

Another example is that Tippu appointed a pathan to plunder the wealth of local Kodavas. The pathan used to loot the wealth along with the soldiers. The local who were fed up with his atrocities killed him on a hill near Polibetta in Veerajpet Taluk. Tippu who came to know of this captured locals and punished them severly. He constructed a masjid in memory of such a thug in Polibetta village. That masjid is named after Pathan Baba and the local muslims conduct urus every year. These things prove that Tippu was more interested in promoting his follower Pathan rather than responding to the problems of local people.

If Tippu had been a patriot, he would have taken the support of Nizam of Hyderabad, Marathas and the local Kodavas in driving out the British. Why did he take the support of French and Khalifa? Why did he cunningly attack the local people who were gathered in Devatta Prarambu playground? Why did he appoint Frenchman Monsent Lali as incharge of Kodagu? All these questions raise serious doubts.

There is no doubt that Tippu was an excellent administrator. But it is difficult to conclude whether he was anti-Hindu or religious tolerant or a blind follower of Islam.

Tippu had devoted most of his time for the propagation of Islam and elimination of Kafirs. He had written to the king of Afghanistan Zaman Sha, the translated version of which has been recorded by writer Kabir Kousal. It reads: "We have to fight unitedly against the enemies of our religion. Waging religious war is my ambition". Going by the gist of the letter it is clear that he was more interested in encouraging his nawabs and soldiers rather than his love for his religion.

After the victory of Mangalore war he converted thousands of Christians to Islam. Those who declined were dragged to Srirangapatna where they were subsequently subjected to harassment.

Similarly, he put down the rebellion of Nairs and forcibly converted them to Islam. This clearly tells that Tippu indulged in forcible conversion to all those who came in his way of Digvijaya. Even today, we find such Christian families in Dhakshina Kannada district and Nair communities in Malabar region. Considering all these, we may come to the following conclusion.

## CONCLUSION

My opinion is that Tippu was neither a patriot nor anti-British. He was also not anti- Hindu or religious tolerant. He was not even a staunch follower of Islam. He was an opportunist and a shrewd administrator besides being a statesman. We cannot simply attribute patriotism to him just because he opposed British. Though he opposed British, he developed friendship with the French. It is pertinent to know that the French had been defeated by the British in Europe and hence they could not establish theirs colonies in India firmly. They would have established their colonies in India had the British not come here.

If he were to be a staunch follower of Islam, Why did he consider Nizam of Hyderabad as his enemy as the latter was also a Muslim? That clearly shows that conversion was one of the strategies adopted by Tippu to suppress his opponents. To conclude, Tippu was not only an astute politician but also a matured statesman.

# REFERENCES

[1]  P. S. Appaiah, A History of Kodagu, 2012.

[2]  B. D. Ganapathy, Kodavas, Jyothi Prakashana, Temple Road, Madikeri, 1980.S

[3]  Krishna Iyer L. A., The Coorg Tribes and Castes, Madras, 1948.

[4]  Muthanna I. M., A Tiny Model State of South India, Poly Betta, Coorg, 1953.

[5]  Moogling H., Coorg Memoirs, Bengaluru, 1855.

[6]  Muthanna Pandanda, Coorg and the Coorgs, 1931.

[7]  Muthanna I. M., The Coorg Memoirs, Deepak, Mysuru, 1971.

[8]  Richter G., A Manual of Coorg – A Gazetteer, Delhi, 1870.

[9]  Richter G., Ethnographical Compendium on the Castes and Tribes found in the Province of Coorg, Bengaluru, 1887.

[10] Rice Lewis B., Mysore and Coorg Gazetteer, Vol. III, Bengaluru, 1878.

[11] Subbaiah K. K., Archealogy of Coorg, Mysuru, 1978.

[12] B. N. Satyan, Coorg District Gazetteer, Bengaluru, 1975(Ed).

[13] Rice, Epigraphia Carnatica, Edn Revised, Vol. I, Coorg District, 1914(Ed).

[14] B. L. Rice, Epigraphia Carnatica, Vol. IX, 1905.

[15] Dr. B. S. Kulakarni, Indian Chronological Tables, Karnataka University, 1977.

[16] Bar Association Virajpet Kodagu 1968-1998, Souvenir Centenary Celebrations of Virajpet Courts, 1998.

[17] Javare Gowda D., A Study of Village Names of Mysore Districts, Dejagow Trust,      Kalanilaya, Jayalaxmi Puram, Mysore

[18] Poojanda S. Appaiah, Kodava English Dictionary, 2010.

[19] P. T. Bopanna, The Romance of Indian Coffee, Prism Books Press, Bangalore, 2011.

[20] P. T. Bopanna, Coorg Land of beauty and Valor, 2010

# Kaimada the Unique culture of Kodava Society

*Dr. Lalitha K. P.*

Kaimada means ancestor - shrine. The Kodavas who erected these Kaimadas have left no written documents or evidence, explaining how and why they had gone about making them.

Early accounts-

When questioned, elders explained that the Kaimadas are tombs of the founder of the Okka, Okka property, and his wife. He is referred to as moolapurusha [original man] or aadi guru [first preceptor], or aadiKaarona [first ancestor],

There is no exact date that states as to when these structures were erected. We believe that the first Kaimada was built at Baithuur and Payyauur. Where their leader or "Thakkas" were buried.'Baithuur' means abode and 'Achha' means father. Etymologically 'BaithuurAchha' means "father is in heaven". When we closely observe we can find steep-sloped stepped Kaimadas. The structure of these Kaimadas to some extent resembles the Pyramids.

Finding East-West and North-south direction.

To find out the direction North and South, the planers may have used the Sun, to find North. A pole was set in the ground, with a weighted string attached. This weighted string hung straight down and was used to make sure that the pole was upright. The pole's morning shadow was marked as a line on the ground and used to make a circle. As the Sun crossed the sky, the shadow shrink until midday and then lengthened in the afternoon.

When the shadow touched the circle again, it was marked as a second line. By halving the angle between the two lines, kodava planners could find North. The Kaimada was built within the sight of the Sun and the Moon Gods. The founder of the property of Okka was believed to be a God on Earth who hoped to join the Sun God after death.

Kaimadas always oriented along the four cardinal directions. So the first task to find the precise location of the North—South line on the ground to form one side of the Kaimada's square base. They would then lay out the Kaimadas' other Sides.

The instrument Kodavas used to create the perfect square was far less sophisticated than those used today. The line of the bases was probably measured using, wooden pegs and long creepers or ropes. From the square base, an earthen platform would be raised to the height of 3 feet or 5 feet above the ground level then the dead body of "Kaarana" and his wife "Korthi" [another name Panjuruli] would be buried in the center of the square placing the head to the South and the legs to the North. After some time a 3 feet square gopuram like structure would be raised from where the chest and head are placed. A door like opening is made facing East and all the other areas covered with walls. When the walls reach the height of 5 feet from that square, four sloping sides would be built up to meet at one point. These four sloping sides have three steps like structure representing the Kodava belief on the Sun, the Moon, and the Earth. On the second step, they used to carve a crescent moon-like symbol. So the whole Kaimada would serve as a launchpad, to send Kaarana and Korthi into the sun god.

In earlier days it seems they might have used earthen blocks to raise the platform and also to build the walls and gopuram like structure at the center of the square. Gradually around the earthen platforms, odd stone walls or thorikall [soft stone] blocks were constructed to give more strength and longevity to the platform. In the hallowed chamber,

Kodavas always keep a lit earthen lamp and offerings made to "Kaarana" and "Korthi". Kodavas believe that fire is the son of the Sun god. Which is why the sacred lamp is lit and saluted in the morning and the evening.

Kodavas believe that they are lords of the three lokas namely Surya loka, Chandra loka, and Bhuloka. Depending on the occasions and ceremonies Kodavas wear red vastra on head or golden bordered mandaethuni or red mandaethuni, - symbol of Surya, white kupya (over coat) - a symbol of the Moon, and blue sash - a symbol of the Earth. But now it has changed to golden bordered mandaethuni (Turbon), white shirt, and black colored kupya that represents their courage, etc.

In many religions around the world, fire is taken as a witness in ceremonies. In the Kodava community fire is taken as a witness. The sacred fire is never allowed to die out. There was also the practice of trial by fire, in which the innocent would be unharmed, while the guilty would perish. Fire is believed to be a symbol of justice, truth, and purity.

The religious belief of the Kodavas, proposed the existence of one supreme god—Paramathma or Para Brahmma or Bhagavantha and so on. The creator of the Universe is omnipotent, omnipresent, and omniscient. The visible Sun god is the most important God to Kodavas. So the Kaimadas and Ainmanae (Ancestors House) were built facing East towards the rising sun.

Ancient Kodava's ideas about life and death were complex. Every one thought life is to be made of Panchabhutha or elements, namely Earth, Water, Fire, Air, and Sky. All these elements are different forms of the same existential energy, we call Gods, that are need to be protected.

It is believed that there are two forms of the spirit the jeewa and the kuuli, the jeewa is the life force that needs food to survive. A Kaarana'sjeewa could enter his Kaimada and receive food offerings on his behalf. The kuuli represents his ability to move around. So Kaarana'sjeewa even though separated from his body could move from buried body high up in his Kaimada or travel up towards the stars. At the moment of death, Jeewa, Kuuli (Spirit) and body are believed to separate. They are brought together during the funeral rituals. The jeewa and Kuuli are now united as a third spirit, which is shining light in both the Devaloka and Kaimada.

When a Kodava dies, the people of the community believed that the deceased individual would travel up to the sky and join the gods. Fireballs would be shot up in the air during ancient days and now firing a gunshot to the sky symbolizes that a jyothi is left the earth to the sky to join the gods. These are also in the forms of funeral songs that the Kodavas call chaavupaat and polchhipaat. It is believed that after death Kaarana leaps up into the sky as a crow or an owl, it is helped by winds and storms to reach the 'afterlife'. A gold coin is placed on the forehead which symbolizes that the Kaarana reached the Swarga Loka with a Sun's disc. To reach the new life it is said that the Kaarana has to pass through a pair of doors at the point on the Eastern horizon where the Sun rises each day. The ancient Kodavas believe that this was where the new life begins. The kaimadastructure declared that the double doors of the horizon are opened on his journey to the afterlife - the Kaarana was reborn as a spirt king of the dead of the Okka. While the dead kaarana become the spirit, his eldest son on Earth replaced him as the new form of the head of Okka.

Kaarana was served in the afterlife by the elders in the Okka, who performed rituals in his honor both in Ainmanae and in Kaimada. During the earlier days, the Kodavas believed that Kaarana needed three meals a day, two in the sky, and one on the Earth. Accordingly, food was offered to the Sun in the morning, to the Earth at noon and night to the Moon.

Kaarana watched over the Okka land, making sure that the crops would grow in the field and that the Sun and the Moon carried on its daily journey across the sky. Safe in Kaimada, Kaarana was now united with the Sun and the Moon gods. High up in his burial chamber, he would be close to the Sun's and Moon's rays. Meanwhile - the elders in the Okka kept his memory alive by performing their daily rituals.

During festivals like Kailpaud, Puthhari festival, and a marriage, a little meat curry and rice are offered on a plantain leaf to the ancestors. A leaf —cup of toddy or arrack is also kept on the plantain leaf. The ancestors consume the essence of the offering and thereby consecrate it. All food or any article which has been offered to Kaarana is called meedi (prasaada) Quite apart from festivals and other occasions when the dishes cooked in the house are offered to the ancestors before the members themselves partake of them, there are special occasions when the ancestors have to be offered food and drink, and these occasions are the last days (changraandi) of the months of Taurus and Cancer, and the tenth of Libra. The propitiation of ancestors once in a year or two years with non - vegetarian food and liquor and bolque (lights) sacrifice of pig and fowls is called kaaranaBharani. There is also a more elaborate propitiation of ancestors called Kaaranathaerae or Kaarana koala, at which Maliyas or Bannas officiate as priests and oracles. The propitiation is invariably performed at the ancestral house. The latter is whitewashed, and the floors washed with a solution of cow-dung. Nowadays the head of the Okka (Pattadaar) writes a letter to the heads of the branches living elsewhere, and to other relatives, informing them of the date of the propitiation.

On the appointed day they all gather together at the ancestral house, bringing their votive offerings (parkae) of fowl or pig or both along with them. A daughter of the house who has married out might bring with her a votive animal to a Kaarana of her natal Okka.

The propitiation begins sundown. Everyone takes a bath, and the head of the Okka dresses in a waist-cloth and shoulder-cloth. If he is very pious he even observes a fast. The Bannas or Maliyas perform the propitiatory ritual in the central hall of the ancestral house. One of the Bannas or Maliyas acts as an oracle (Thirolakaara or bolchapaad) while another, or two others, beat drums and sing the Okka song of the propitiating Okka. The song gives us an account of the life of each ancestor and ancestors. At present in Kodagu most of the Okkas have discontinued this practice. Although, there is no uniform rule as to when the propitiation should be performed; each Okka seems to follow a different rule in this matter.

Before a particular ancestor leaves him, the oracle goes to the Kaimada or ancestor - shrine, where one of his party sacrifices a fowl or pig. Liquor, parched rice, coconut, and plantains are all offered to the ancestor represented by the oracle. He gets ready to impersonate the next ancestor named by the 'Pattadaara' or head of the okka.

Then follows the ancestors 'Kanithaayi' (kaarana's wife) oracle who wears a traditional koarikodae (umbrella) inspects the entire paddy field and returns. Then follows alue - thalaeyakkithaayi oracle (ancestral mothers of each linage for over seven generations), then nuurpadivandakodchchi and Muupa (centenarians) Kodchchithaai and kodibeeranga (women and men who gave up their lives for a cause). If a mother and a baby suffer from any illness, the parents in the family make up their mind to arrange thaerae of kani - thaai and kodchchithaayi, which is at recent times not being practiced. In case there was any kind of vow the Kodavas used to arrange Naripuuda during ancestral worship.

The last ancestor to possess the oracle is the Founder, in whose honor the oracle wears the upper part of his thaerae equipment. The Kaarana-thaerae may demand to be shown around the paddy - field to see for himself whether it is looked after properly. Thus a Kodava continues to take an interest in the affairs of his Vakka even after his death, which means that he continues to care for the paddy-field on which the prosperity and happiness of the Vakka and thus, indirectly, of the total society depends. A pig is usually sacrificed to the founder. The head of the Okka requests the Founder to bless the descendants.

On the next morning the sacrificed animals are cooked and the entire village is invited to dinner. Thus an ancestor - propitiation is also an occasion for the expression of the solidarity of the village. The Bannas or the Maliyas get as their perquisites the heads of the animals sacrificed, provisions, some cooked meat, and also a little cash.

Even today several prosperous and well-known okkas have no Kaimadas. But originally, odd stones embedded in earthen platforms round the milk exuding trees seem to have represented the ancestors everywhere in Kodagu. These places were called KaaranaKoata and later on started to call KaaranaKott.

The period of ritual mourning for those who observe kuliquenippad ends with the thueekaeuththuva or adpa ceremony at the confluence of the Cauvery at Bhagamandala. On Cauvery changrandi or kirusankramana they have to go to Cauvery or one of the holy places on the banks of river Cauvery. Men should shave their heads and beards and women should remove their nipputhuni bathe in the river and offer pinda in the name of the departed soul. When they go to Cauvery to perform thueekaeadpa ritual they should carry two silver figurine of the deceased person, puja needs to be performed at the Bhagandeshwara temple and at Thala Cauvery they must put one silver figurine to the holy ktmdigae. Then holy water known as theertha is collected and brought home. Another silver figurine is immersed in the Thala Cauvery and brought home. Then they sprinkle the holy water in and around the house and the house is now believed to be sanctified.

Earlier people believed that when one of the silver figurines was put into the holy kundigae at Thala Cauvery the departed soul would go straight to heaven. In earlier days people would wait for a minimum of 48 days i.e one mandala to a maximum of one year, before offering pinda, because it was believed that otherwise the soul would not find salvation. Today, again due to the constraint of time and the distant place of living, people observe this ritual within a week of the maada.

The other silver figurine they used to keep in a wooden box which is already kept in the kaimada. The total number of silver figurines in the wooden box helped the Vakka people to get a picture of the number of generations passed away and total number of deaths in the family. But after Tipu's invasion some of these practices died down, some Vakka even today maintaining the family tree and in some other Vakka, efforts are being made to revive it.

Ten days after Cauvery changrandi, the ritual of pathhalodi [kaarananguemeedibeppa] is performed. The Vakka members invite all the blood relatives for this ceremony. The silver figurine would now be placed in the kaimada and meedi is kept.

The Kodavas used to erect a bamboo pole in front of the Kaimada near their aynmanae. It was meant for suggesting happy and inauspicious occasions in the family at different times. The erection of this pole was called KODIMARA. It used to be a straight and neat stick. It measures ten feet in length. This pole was being decorated in many ways; and each of which suggested to others the nature of the occasion in the family. The symbol of wishing a happy meeting was indicated by tying a bunch of pepper and a twig of green leaves to the Kodimara and it was called santhaanavriksha. Similarly a victory in war was indicated by tying of colourful quill of birds to the Kodimara, and at the top of it, a white cloth - sheet flew fluttering. If the cloth was torn at the center, it implied that good relations between two localities were affected. It was called kudikuutva. If the individual good relation was at stake the bunch of pepper was split and tied to Kodimara. If lovers lost their concern to each other, Kodavas used to split the betel leaves and tie them to the pole [kodiyalaekeethva] Similarly the dry bald pole indicated death in the family. Likewise, if bunches of Nukki leaves and Neem leaves had been tied to the kodimara, it indicated an attack of epidemics like small - pox in the family.

## Bibliography


1. Mysore and Coorg. Vol. III - Coorg. Editor - Benjamin Lewis Rice
2. Gazetteer of Coorg. - G. Richter
3. A study of the Origins of Coorgs by Lt. Col. K.C. Ponnappa - 1997.
4. The Coorgs and their Origins by M.P. Cariappa and PonnammaCariappa - 1981.
5. Kodavas and their Gala and Lela - by I.M. Muthanna - 1987.
6. Archaeology of Coorg by Dr. K.K. Subbayya - 1978.
7. Caste and Tribes of south India - Edgar Thuston - 1909.
8. Religion and Society among the Coorgs of South India - by M.N. Srinivas - 1951.

# The Extinct Tribes of Kodagu District

*Dr. Lalitha K. P.*

## ABSTRACT

This document gives a study of the extinct tribes in Coorg (Kodagu), a district in Karnataka state, India. In this paper an attempt has been made to discuss various aspects of life of tribes in Coorg. An analysis of Social Life of tribal people in Coorg has been done with an emphasis on their customs and traditions like marriage, status of women etc.

**Keywords:** Coorg, Kodagu, Kodava.

## INTRODUCTION

The diversity and variety and of course, the underlying unity of India is obvious. These people of each region of this vast land of the Indian Union have certain distinctive strands and features-in face and figure, food and dress, language and literature, faculties and traits. Therefore each region has some uniqueness of its own. Yet a common culture binds the people of India together. India extending from Kanyakumari in the south to the Himalayas in the north is the motherland of the Indians. In this vast tract of land, Kodagu is a very tiny spot, which had once the status of a state and now forms a district of Karnataka.

The Coorg tribes are entirely different from the other communities of South India. They have their own unique social customs. Their dress and ornaments do not have anything in common with what is generally known as typically South India. During the Vedic period the Aryans had established themselves in North India and the Dravidians in the South. The great epic Ramayana is said to be roughly 500 years (3000 B.C.) old. The story of Kodagu is even more ancient. Its soil was sanctified by Sri Rama both on his way to

---

Lanka and on his return from there. The people of Kodagu worshipped Rama even from the Ramayana times. There is a sacred spot called 'Iruppu' in the village of 'Kurchi' in South Kodagu on the Brahmagiri hills, where there is a temple of Rama. The Ramatirtha stream and the Lakshmanatirtha river take their sources on one range of the Brahmagiri hills; and, on another in North Kodagu, the Kaveri takes her source.

## KODAGU THROUGH THE AGES FROM THE VEDIC PERIOD TO THE PRESENT DAY – CHRONOLOGICAL TABLE

- Vedic period:
  Aryans in the North and Dravidians in the South
  The Era of the Great Epic Ramayana – About 2000 B.C.

- Later Vedic Period:
  Migration of Indo-Aryans to the South – 600 B.C.

- Gangas of Gangavadian Talakad – 100 to 980 A.D.

- Earlier Kadambas of Banavasi and Halsi – 450 to 560 A.D.

- Early Chalukyas of Vatapi ( Badami )
          : Pulikesin II – 630 A.D.
          : Vikramaditya I – 654 A.D.

- Pandyas of Madurai: Maravarman Rajasimha I – 730 to 765 A.D.

- Cholas – 985 to 1176 A.D. and Earlier Changalas – 1034 to 1249 A.D.

- Kongalvas of Shanivarasanthe and Arkalgud – 1004 to 1176 A.D.

- Hoysalas of Belur and Dvarasamudra – 1116 to 1300 A.D.

- Kongalvas – 1034 to 1297 A.D.

- Hoysalas – 1116 to 1300 A.D. and Earlier Changalvas of Chenganad –1034 to 1297 A.D.

- Later Chalukyas of Vatapi ( Badami ) – 1050 to 1192 A.D.

- Nava Dannayakas of Gundlupet – 1300 to 1321 A.D.

- Vijayanagar Kingdom – Between 1390 and 1565 A.D. and Petty Cheiftains called Nayakas.

- Later Changalvas – From the end of the 14th century to 1644 A.D.

- Belur Nayakas – 17th century

- Kodava Nayakas – 1600 to 1633

- Haleri Rajas – 1600 to 1834
- British Rule – 1834 to 1947

## STATES REORGANISATION: Kodagu became a district of Karnataka, 1956

What is unique about Kodagu and its tribes? Pre – historic dolmens or burial cairns were found in Kodagu as in other parts of South India. Though these cairns throw some light on the life of those pre-historic people, we cannot form an opinion as to who they were – whether the remains form an opinion as to who they were, whether the remains that are found were the Coorgs or that of the original inhabitants of the tract of land like Yeravas, Holeyas, Kudiyas etc, is not clear.

## SOME OF THE TRIBES OF COORG

## YERAVAS:

They are said to be originally from Wayanad, who were, like the Holeyas in Coorg. They were held in slavery by the Nairs. They are found almost entirely in Kiggatnad and Yedenalknad taluks. They speak a language of their own, a dialect of Malayalam, and live with the Coorgs, but always in separate huts or near the jungle. They are much sought after as Labourers. They appear to be treated much as slaves, and features: have thick lips and a compressed nose, and are very scantily clothed. At their weddings and their pandal – ata or demon feast, they chant their peculiar songs, and have dances in which, as with the Paleyars, their women take part. They disguise as Panjaras and Paniyara in dense masses which are never disturbed by a comb: their appearance is most extraordinary, like that of the Australian Papua. The Paniyas Yeravas appear more civilized.

## KURUBA (Shepherd):

This caste consist Kambli Kurubas and Hal Kurubas. There are also other classes of Kurubas, called Betta, Jenu and Kadu Kurubas; but these latter classes are distinguished from the two former by being classed among the wild tribes.

The Kambli and Hal Kurubas live in the villages, whereas the others, as their names denote, live in the forests and jungles. The two former are also known by the name Ooru (Village) Kurubas. It seems doubtful whether there are so many Ooru Kurubas as the number shown in the statement, viz., 687. Of this number 174 are labourers, 6 agriculturists, 7 domestic servants and 17 who came under the head of manufacturers or Kambli-makers. They worship all kinds of idols, stones, trees and evil spirits.

## UPPAR:

The Uppars as the name implies , were originally a caste occupied in making salt . Now they engage in bricklaying and carpentry and about a third of the whole number have been returned as labourers. The total number of males are 83 while females being 16.

## PEGGADES(heggades)

They immigrant cultivators from Kerala and are found all over the Province, but chiefly in Yedenalknad and Padinalknad. Like the Aimmokkalu, they conform to Coorg customs, but are equally excluded from the community of the Coorgs, in whose presence they are allowed to sit only on the floor, while the former occupy a chair. The Peggades speak Coorgi.

## KAVATI:

They are not a numerous class and are found in Yedenalknad. They resemble the Coorgis in language and dress and are said to have come originally from Kerala.

## MARTA:

These are a small class in Coorg. Their number is probably understated, as they generally call themselves Smarta Brahmans, though no Brahman will recognize them. They are almost confined to Yedenalknad taluk.

**DOMBAS:**

They are a class of professional wrestlers, tumblers and beggars. They are Shudras from the north of India and speak a dialect of their own, similar to Hindustani. They are found in small parties scattered all over Coorg and Mysore.

**MALEYAS:**

They are a small wandering tribe of gipsies from Malabar, who speak Malayalam. They pretend to cure diseases and extract money from the ignorant.

**KANIYAS:**

They are said to be the descendents of a Malayalam Brahman and a lower caste woman.

A FEW UNIQUE CUSTOMS FOUND IN THESE TRIBES.

JAMMA ------ a land tenure.

There is a special system of land tenure in Kodagu known as the Jamma. This special land tenure Jamma means birth under which most of the Kodavas who held their land were bestowed on them by Rajas ensuring their military allegiance. It was a hereditary right passing from father to son and for that reason was called Jamma which meant birth. This special tenure was exclusively bestowed on the Kodava community though there may be Jamma holders of other communities whose number may be negligible and who got it by virtue of service to the king. The objective of the bestowal on the Kodava community was to ensure their help in times of war. The Jamma tenure was a light one in terms of money being only half of the rate of the Sagu land. People holding Jamma lands were liable to be called upon for military service. According to Rev. G. Richtor who wrote "A manual of Coorg", the Jamma ryots are still liable to be called out to repel outward aggression and quell internal disturbances, to furnish all police and treasure guards etc. during peace time. Jamma tenure was of advantage in view of not only the economic benefit but also of local prestige. It signified that the holder was the son of the soil having deep roots in Kodagu land.

## KUDAVALI MANGALA:

There are three varieties of Kudavali (living together) marriages viz ., the marriage of the widow with one of the brothers of the late husband, marriage of the widow with a man of a different family and marriage of a divorced woman. Usually 'Kudavalis' are contacted due to the exigencies of the family, or of the children. These marriages are simple ceremonies and lack the pomp and gaiety of the 'Kannimangala'. The widow can marry one of the brothers of the dead husband and continue in the same family or she can marry one of the cousin brothers of the deceased husband. According to this kind of marriage the groom will observe all the customs of a 'Kannimangala' and will perform the 'Muhurtha'. For the bride this being the second marriage she will have no 'Muhurtha', for according to the kodava custom a woman can have only one regular marriage whereas the man is entitled for more.

## KUDAVALI WITH ONE OUTSIDE THE FAMILY:

If the widow intends to marry a person outside her conjugal family, first she has to sever her connection with it and return to her natal family. The custom of severing the connection is called 'Kallumara Kaipo'. According to this the '*Aruva*' of the bride's natal family with two of its members and the '*Aruva*' of the late husband's family with at least one or two people not belonging to the family must be present at the function. The ritual is performed in the central hall of the house. The boxes and things which the widow brought at her marriage should be kept there. The presence of the widow is considered as not necessary.

## KUDAVALI OF A DIVORCEE:

There is only a slight difference in this 'Kudavali' specially in the custom of severing the connection to the late husband's family . But according to this custom it is not decent that she should contact another marriage before the lapse of at least six months.

## OKKA PARIJE:

If in a family there is only one unmarried girl and no heir, the girl is married according to *'okka parije'* by which the children of the marriage become members of their mother's natal family. The man who marries her ceases to be a member of the wife's family. This arrangement is made so that the family should not become extinct.

## MAKKA PARIJE:

This marriage takes place only for the rights of the children. In the event of there being no male in a family, a daughter is maintained to represent the name of the family and a husband is procured for her. This husband does not become a member of her family as in *'okka parije'* , nor does he become alienated from his own family but can take a wife for his own family thus raising the seed for both the families . The children of *'Makka parije'* have rights of inheritance only in their mother's family.

The husband need not stay permanently at the house of the *'Makka parije'* wife but should visit her and help her in raising the required progeny to perpetuate the family. During his stay the wife is expected to provide him with food and clothing. This is known as *'obbangala'*. The wife should maintain herself and the husband will have no responsibility of providing for her. The husband will have no right over the properties of the wife.

## KUTTA PARIJE:

If an unmarried girl becomes pregnant and if the man who caused pregnancy does not agree to marry her (bendu parije) or the woman or man dies after childbirth, and if the head of the family of the man has no objection to give the child or the widow the rights of the family of the man, that can be done on the day of the death itself before the elders of the family and villagers. The formality of bestowing slightly differs according to the occasion.

There is a special kind of marriage based primarily on superstition and this need not have a bride!

If a married woman dies without children, the parents of the woman or the other members of the natal family can claim from her conjugal family the jewels, trousseau and other things given to her at the time of her marriage.

A widow or a divorced wife can return to the natal family for shelter but she is entitled for food and clothing only but will not have any other rights.

## CONCLUSION

These unique tribes have very rich folk culture and art; unfortunately they are in the brim of extinction, for which the government and the society should show concern towards these tribes and it is their responsibility to help them flourish as for India is well known for the variety of cultures it has.

# REFERENCES

[1] D. N. Krishnaih, History of Coorg, Prasaganga, University of Mysuru.

[2] Ephigraphiya Karnatika Kodagu Jille – Volume 1, Kannada Adhyayana Samsthe, University of Mysuru.

[3] Dr. P.S. Ramanujam, Kodavaru, Prasaranga, Mysuru, 1975.

[4] Chief editor Hampana, Aimamuttanna, Kodava Kannada Nighantu, Karnataka Sahitya Parishattu, Bengaluru.

[5] Edited by Tambanda Vijay Poonachcha, Kodagu Vivarane, Prasaranga, Kannada University, Hampi.

[6] V.N. Nayak, Kodagina Bhougolika Sameekshe, Deepak Prakashana, Goni Koppalu, South Kodagu.

[7] Edited by N.S. Devi Prasad, Kodaginalli Bhasha Samskritika Samarasya, Amara Kranti Utsava Samiti, Sulia, Dakshina Kannada.

[8] Chief editor Baragooru Ramachandrappa, Upa Samskriti Adhyayana Maaleya Pustakagalu, Karnataka Sahitya Academy, Nripatunga Road, Bengaluru.

[9] Tambanda Vijay Poonachcha, Adhunika Kodagu

# Social Structure and Functions of Ancient and Medieval Kodagu

- *Dr. Lalitha K. P.*

Kodagu is a small district in Karnataka state and has the 19th place in land area. Geographically speaking the whole district lies between north latitude 11.56' and 12.52' and East latitude 72.22' and 76.12'. When Kodagu was a Desha, Sulliya Puttur and Periyapattana taluks were included but due to some political and social factors these taluks wre separated from Kodagu Desha and wre included in Dakshina Kannada and Mysore districts. Even Baitoor and Payyauoor were also separated from Kodagu and were included in Kerala state.

Kodagu is a beautiful hill country, most of which is between 3000 and 4000 feet above sea level, though the highest point is around 6000 feet.

It is probable that when these army units entered to Kudumalae desha only eight Thaqqas survived and built the country, other four might have died in Kerala, and their family names are (1) Kallae-Kallaera, (2) Bollae-Bollaera, (3) Kuduva-Kuduvanda, (4) Buduva-Buduvanda, (5) Paandi-Paandira, (6) Parda-Pardanda, (7) Poarae -Poaraera (8) Yeruva -Yeruvanda and other four family names of the Thaqqa's (Thahaqqas) who have died in Kerala are (1) Pugga,,-Puggaera, (2)Bowa-Boweranda, (3)Mundiya-Mundiyolanda (4) Koluva-Koluvanda.

## KEMBATTI POLIYAS.

The Kembatti poliyas came from Kerala and were called as 'Pariahs' in Kerala. If we study carefully the traditional social structure and functions, the apex of the social pyramid occupied by Brahmins (Namputhiris), below them the Nayars, Kurichiyas, below them the Ezhavas and the bottom

---

most place occupied by the pariahs (untouchables and unapproachables). The laws of pollution laid down that a Pariah should not come anywhere near the Namputhiri at all and if they want to convey a message to a Namputhiri was asked to maintain 36 feet distance, should keep 24 feet away from the Nair, and 12 feet away from the Ezhava. This meant that it was in Kerala that the caste system developed its most appalling features. The social pyramid was an economic one too. For, in a feudal society, the top social strata were also the most affluent and represented the land owning groups. The upper crust of Kerala society, thus, was an excessively privileged one. It is no wonder that the land looked like a lunatic asylum to Vivekananda when he visited Kerala.

In Kodagu these Pariah's are called as Poliya's and it is only a phonetic difference between Malayalam and Kodava languages and it seems that Kembatti —poliyas and Yarvas too came from Wayanaad of Kerala along with Kodavas to Kodimalae naad during ending part of third century B.C. or beginning of second century B.C. The Dravidians who came along with Kodavas are represented by Kembatti — poliyas and Yaravas of Wayanaad of Kerala. Some authors opine that the Kembatti's are the indigenous people. Their sacred dress Kembatt kuppya and mundu (waist cloth) are red colour cloth. During their annual festival the Chaundi oracles and other oracles wear red colour kuppya and mundu. Their Gods and Goddesses are fond of blood, so the Chaundi oracles cut their crown of the head and chest and back with jingle sword called kadthalae. The blood which flows from the wound, collects on body as well as on the kuppya and mundu. These blood stained clothes are also called as Kembatt. This explanation I got from vakka elders and my father because our Vakka is also Battyath Vakka of Kunjeri urr Kembatti poliyas shrine or Koata is near the Mundanda Vakka.

In ancient and medieval period they were attached to some Kodava families and villages, so they carried the name of that Vakka or village. Every kembatti poliyas family or village name carry suffix Kuttada means permanent servents attached to that family or village or bonded labourers of a particular family or village.

Another meaning of Kutta is funeral pyre. In ancient and medieval period in Kodagu it was the responsibility of Kembatti poliyas to keep a vigil in crematorium, after setting fire to the dead body of his masters family, till all the firewood become burning cinders.

They are generally of middle size and of a dark complexion. They eat whatever they get, beef also included.

They speak Kodava language and follow customs, dress, rituals such as birth, pollusion, marriage, death rituals, remarriage, festivals like puththari, kailpaud, cauvery—changraandi, agriculture and host of other customs. Their master, servent relationship is of milk and water relationship.

In Kodava marriage after dampathi-muurtha to establish sammanda parajae, the bride is given the rights in the groom's Vakka, bride's aruva asks groom's aruva do you give her, ten units of labourers (husband, wife and children), ie is pathth kudi aalue, Pallilue thonda ie is an aged Kembtti — poliya, Kuuraelue — Muupa, ie is an old Yarava. For this the groom's aruva says yes.

After that the wedding procession crosses the courtyard, an aged Kembatti -Poliya holding a ?aming torch (thuud), spreads a red vasthra in front of them saying that he would not allow the child of his master's house to be taken away. He is given one pana (three anas) to remove the obstruction. It shows the responsibility and obligation of the servents to safeguard and protect the family members and property of his master.

Till recently it was an obligation of Kembatti—poliyas of the Vakka or village to perform the funeral dance (angakali) in the courtyard of the funeral house. A Kembatti — poliya or polthi who performed funeral dance he/ she must observe the Kodava custom of mengathae ippa — mourning rites which is observed by close relatives of the deceased. On the day of maada he/ she brings a basket, filled with some rice, green grain and vegetables to the maada house. This basket is returned to him or she filled with rice, coconut, salt, meat and some oil. On the day of funeral who performed angakali (funeral dance) he/ she is given sufficient white cloth for a kuppya or saree and piece of cloth for nippuque thLuli(shoulder cloth). Formerly, a man and women from the servent family or families observed ritual mourning for their dead master or mistress. The bond between master and servent was strong enough to find expression in rituals.

In Kodava folklore there are instances of a servent's great loyalty to his master and of the latter's great affection for the former. Achchu Kotta, a Kembatti poliya servent of Kallumaadanda Ayyanna, threw himself on the funeral pyre of his master. Ayyanna was very ill when a caravan from Beanguur village set out for Malabar, and Achchu Kotta joined this caravan against his master's wishes. Before the caravan had crossed into Malabar, Achchu Kotta heard that his master had died. Torn with grief and remorse, Achchu Kotta ran back to Beanguur to see the ?ames of the funeral pyre consuming the body of his dead master. Without a second thought Achchu Kotta jumped into the pyre. The members of the Kallurnaadanda Vakka erected a stone in memory of Achchu Kotta outside their Kaimada (ancestor shrine). When an ancestor - propitiation is held in the Kallumaadanda Vakka, offerings of food and drink are made to Achchu Kotta's stone also.

When a Kembatti poliya does a piece of work, the mistress of the house gives him a small quantity of castor oil in addition to the kochchi (wages) paid in paddy or rice and nuchchi (broken rice). The application of castor oil to the head is supposed to have a 'cooling' effect on the entire body. Hard work, especially in the sun, brings about 'heat' in the body which needs to be 'cooled' by the application of castor oil to the head. The giving of castor oil by the mistress shows her concern for the health and well being of the servent; it is an act of friendship.

Till the end of medieval period in Kembatti community, after the marriage of a boy comes to his masters Vakka house touches the feet of elders, then the girl carry a basket which is filled with cow-dung and dumps the same to a paddy plot. This is an evidence to prove that there was no untouchability system between them.

In most of the Kodagu villages exist Kembatti poliyas shrines or there is a place dedicated in a jungle under some big tree to their gods and goddesses. Their shrines are called Koata, and to manage them and to organize festivals (nammae) once in a year, there are Kodava Battiyath Vakkas (management family). Their worship is addressed to Ayyappa, Kari— chaundi, Puli — chaundi (kaali) and kumda. They sacrifice a pig, or a goat, fowl and occasionally he buffalo. There is no priesthood attached to these shrines but the head of few Kodava Battiyath Vakkas in the village officiates as a priest and prays to the god, making the necessary offerings.

## MAARANGI POLIYAS.

Maarangi's also came from Wyanaad of Kerala along with Kodawas to Kodimalae naad, and were expert hunters and fighters. They are generally of middle size and of a dark complexion, and spoke Dravidian type of language resemble

Malayalam, but later adopted Kodava language. They accompanied Kodavas to hunt animals in thick forests and showed them the route to return to the place from where they started the game by keeping some indications or marks. For this expertise they were known as Maarangi's. Their traditional dress, customs, rituals, festivals are same as Kodavas. They too have family names as Kembatti poliyas. At present most of them are found in Ammaththi, Devanageri, and Mythaadi villages.

During the rule of Lingayat kings in Kodagu BERERA POONACHA was Kaaryakaara (commander of 100 soldiers) He had a Maarangi servent named Chitti who was also an expert horse rider. The cunning, cruel, and lunatic king could not digest their famousness and valourism, so he decided to finish both of them. So the king ordered to fasten them to Elephant's legs and to drag them around the fort, but they did not die. So they first hit Poonacha's head, with a stick, with uncontrollable pain Poonacha sought the help of his servent, so he uttered the name Chitti ..... ..and died. Then they killed chitti also.This shows the close relationship and attachment between master and servents. Berera Vakka gave a place to Chitti, near their Kaimada and during Paththalodi people make offerings to Chitti also.

## YERAVAS

Yaravas were also originally from Wyanaad, and they were held in slavery by the Nairs. They are strong and diligent. In features and complexion they resemble the Kurubas. They speak their own language a dialect of Malayalam. Their cheekbones are rather high and prominent, short nose and nearly ?at, small eyes, dark and deep set; curly hair and almost wooly, dark colour. They are scantily dressed..

Like Kodavas they eat no beef, therefore rank higher than the Poliyas. At their weddings and at their Pandalaata or dernan feast they chant their peculiar songs and have dances in which women also take part called 'YERAVAAAT'. At present they live in Queggattnaad as Kodava's servents and confirmed to the mode of life and worship of Kodavas.

There are two sections among Yeravas — Panjiris and Paniyas. The former allow their ?eecy hair to grow to dense masses which are never combed, but seldom have more than a few straggling hairs to represent a beard.

## 'PAN I YERAVA'

The Paniyas appear more civilized and call themselves as Paniyas. Each section has a headman who seems also to act as its priest. The Paniya headman is called 'MUUPA'.Their family is nuclear consisting of father, mother and children. Their family is patriarchal, patrilineal and patrilocal, the elderly male is the family head and he continues the family ine through his male children. These people use the word PATTOLAE or THARANA to indicate the lineage of families, and marriage within the Pattolae or Tharana is tabooed.

Their deities are - Thambira, Thambirathi, Anjalattu, Appaemutti, Kaathmuttachi, Neermuttachi, and thithmuttachi. (muttachi means spirit). Among these deities, Thambira, Anjalattu and Appemutti are male deities and the rest are female deities. They have installed these deities in hut temples, which are globe shaped, near their Kuuraes or localities and forests, and deities are in the form of shapeless stones. By the side of the stone deities they keep sword, spear, a lamp,and a bell.

## 'PAN|IRI YERAVA'

Panjiri yeravas have come from Wayanaad to Kodagu, and are found in Parattimalae near Baithuur on the Kerala border. They are greatly influenced by the culture of Kurichiya tribes of Wayanaad particularly the Matriarchal, matrilineal, and matrilocal system of marriage and property. They speak their own tribal language and their phonems are related to Malayaalam language. Their huts called Kuurae is also like that of Kurichias Mittom. (we come across the words Kuurae and Muupa in Kodavas sammanda parajae) Being matriarchal, Panjiri reckon the progeny through their daughters, and children belong to the mother's lineage. Marriage of a Panjiri does not change the lineage of a man or a women. It is noteworthy that eventhough the Panjiri family is matriarchal, the property is managed by maternal uncle like that of Nairs joint family Tarwad, and Kurichiyas family Mittom, also managed by their respective maternal uncles. Senior most maternal uncle assumes the responsibility of arranging events like marriage, death rituals and look after the property of his sisters. The Panjiri lineages are known as chamma or Kudi and children among these people come under mother's chamma. The elderly man in the Chamrna is called Chammakaara, and another name is Kanaladi. Panjiri village is known as Kunja and each kunja is managed by Kunjakaar. They were food gatherers, thenchanged the habit into kumri agriculture, and gradually they have become agricultural labourers

Accodding to their folklore, there are 33 family names, they are Anjila, Badqmanju, Balaepathera, Bellichalu, Bainaatlu, Chaindae, Chalumbeadu, Chaegadi, Cheruvalla, Evila, Aidaemalae, Kachchaelae, Kadaemalae, Kaalakottai, Kallmnaani, Mudrila, Mudunguththu, Naalapaadi, Panneli, Paavadae, Podarmanju, Puudaari, Puducheri, Puduru, Thirumanjae, Ulaanguttu and each family is exogamus.

These people also practice divorce, remarriage, and widow marriage. They bury the dead body and perform obsequies on eleventh day, six months later arrange a gathering to serve food to the people. The Yerava families gather each year in February or March to offer oblations to ancestors in order to seek their blessings.

Their deities are Pukkarimagae, Karchchathaai Maliyammae and Pakathayya. Panjiris woriship their original ancestors viz., Mel Arachai and Keel Arathi. The ancestors have their abode in Wayanaad. There are stones in a ruined temple at Kuduraekodae near Thirunelli, and it is a pilgrimage centre for the Panjiris. Kunjneladi, the priest for the Panjiris invoke the presence of the three Manju (Shiva) deities and worship them. Their temples resemble that of the Pani Yerva's in structure that is round shaped. At home they worship only their ancestors.

## MALAE KUDIYAS.

Malae Kudiyas are hill tribe, originally they were known as 'Kuruvas'and they spoke their own tribal language. They lived by hunting, honey gathering, toddy taping and cultivation of fruit trees on Malabar and Koclagu hills. They are composed of two endogamous groups, namely Uumaalae or Uuru or village Kudiyas and Themalae Kudiyas (honey-gathering Kudiyas). The Uumaalae kudiyas are also known as Puumaalae Kudiyas. Each group claims superiority over the other, with neither inter — dining nor inter — marrying. Cross cousin marriage is in vogue among them. Their disputes are settled by a few elderly members of their community. The elderly men and women are cremated. The Malae Kudias worship the spirits of ancestors. They also worship all kinds of spirits and minor deities called Bhuthas. In the past, they used to have their demon dances and sacrifices in the dark recesses of the forests called 'Malae Thirikae', or jungle shrine, their Bhuthas being Tharnmayya and Malaethampuraan (Malaethambiraan). They are found in hill regions of Kodagu and Kerala border that is in the forests of the Western Ghats. They conform as much as circumstances permit, to the mode of life, dress, dialect, and social and religious customs of the Kodavas to whom they look up as their masters.

They cultivate their own Kumri land, draw toddy from the 'Panae—mara (caryota urens) for sale and work as labourers on Kodava farms and cardamom gardens and live in the outhouses of the Kodavas.

## 'AMMA KODAVAS'

The first Aryan penetration to the deep- south took place during 6th century B.C., and Namputhir s respresent the spearhead of Aryan penetration to the Kerala (Malabar). Vedic Hinduism percolated to the south from very early days, though the religion as well as the associated culture, whose medium was Sanskrit, completely stabilized itself in Kerala only by about the 8th century A.D. In the early phase of linguistic studies in Kerala, the richly sanskritic texture of modern Malayalam prompted one writer to state that the language evolved originally from Sanskrit and blended subsequently with Dravidian currents. They spoke sanskrit and Sanskrit is the classical language of India, with strong affinities to Greek and Latin and rest of the Indo- European tongues. By 8th century A.D., Kerala had 18 academies teaching Vedic lore, the science and philosophy in sanskrit. The Vedic institutions still survive at Trichur and Tirunava. Temples also became centres of learning. The tradition which evolved subsequently of specialized disciplines becoming the hereditary pursuits of particular Namputhiri families who played a great role in maintaining the continuity of culture and its enrichment.

Among Namputhiri philosophers, the Sarmanes are the most honourable ones. They live in the forests and villages, subsist on leaves, wild fruits and milk, wear white apparel and white linen, use skins of fawns or antelopes or tigers; to sleep and to sit. All of them wear long hair and long beards, plait their hair and bind it with a fillet. They communicate with the king and other community leaders who consult them by —messengers regarding causes of things and who through them worship and supplicate the Deity.

Next in honour to the Sarmane's are the physicians, for they apply philosophy to the study of nature of man. They are frugalin their habits but do not live in the fields. Their food consists of rice and barley meal. The remedies in most repute are ointments and plasters.

Both these classes practice fortitude as well by undergoing active toil to endure suffering, so that they will remain motionless for a whole day in one fixed posture. These philosophers well versed in the Vedas, boast themselves as representatives of God and after their death where their bodies are buried people erected temple buildings and started worshipping them.

Namputiri Brahmins joint family is patriarchal, patrilineal, and patrilocal and is called as Illom. Property is impartible and inalienable. This tradition led to the practice of only the eldest Namputhiri male of the younger generation in the family marrying within the community. The younger brothers married Kshatriya girls, but they had no property which their progeny could inherit, since inheritance in the Namputhiri community was confined to the eldest sons through the Namputhiri wives.

The Dravidians who came still late is represented by Nairs. The word Nair seems originally to have meant captaincy in the army. But the protracted war led to the differentiation of the Nair community on the basis of military service. Since it was very close to the ruling house, the community steadily gained in social status.

Brahmin (Namputhiri) youths who could now marry Kshatriya woman could now marry Nair and Kodava girls also. This practice seems to have reached the climax during the 8''' century A.D. where Namputhiri youths married Kodava girls. The inter caste marriage between Namputhiri boys and Kodava girls constituted a separate caste group called "AMMA KOADAVAS" and later they became a separate endogamous group in Kodagu. Men are highly brahminised in their customs and rituals because husband or father is a Namputhiri Brahmin and wife or mother a Kodava gradually adopted to the customs and rituals of Namputhiri Brahmins. Like the Brahmins they wear the sacred thread and observe annual shradha or ancestor - feast at which only vegetarian food is offered to the dead ancestors.

The name of an Amma Kodava man has the suffix 'amma' even though (amma) means 'mother' and is normally a suffix to a woman's name in certain parts of south India. Male members of Amma Kodava carry suffix Ammayya name. For example - Bellammayya, Bollammayya, Govindammayya, Muddammayya and so on. They too have family names as Kodavas. It is said that formerly Amma kodavas who were concentrated in south Kodagu used to claim kinship with a similar group of people in Wayanaad. Lewis Rice says that "Amma coorgs seem to have originally come from Malabar". It is also seems true that 'Appa Kodavas' are the decendants of Kodava man and a Namputhiri Brahmin girl of Wayanaad, daughter of 'Tha_ayikaat Thambiraan', who expelled his daughter from his home as she attained puberty before marriage (Formerely among Brahmins, it was regarded as both sinful and shameful to have in the house an unmarried girl who had attained puberty). There were two Appa Kodava families in Kodagu till 1960, but afterwards they have merged with Kodava community.

There are two gothras among them, the Bharadwaja gothra and Vishvamithra gothra and they marry within the same gothra. In dress, birth, authority, Vakka—parajae, ancestor worship, traditions, pollusion, marriage, death rituals, remarriage, festivals like cauvery changraandi and puththari festivals, structure of the house, agriculture and host of other customs and procedures are same as Kodavas.

Amma kodavas are said to have been the indigenous priestwood from 8th century A.D., are also called as cauvery Brahmins and the same is mentioned in skanda purana. They officiated as priests in temples in Kodagu including cauvery till the time of invasion of Tipu sulthan to Kodagu. The only object of fabrication of skanda purana, Chandra Verma and his shudra kanni, can have is, not to clear up the origin of the indigenous priesthood of Kodagu and Kodavas, but to obscure and bury it under the rubbish of puranic lore, which eludes every historical and sociological investigation.

Heed not the scripture that violate the truth of man and his moral law; nor the words of men Who stand to gain by interpreting them wrong. For the ignorant crowd, yesterday's error Hardens into today's tradition, tomorrow's law.

During the reign of Veera Raja a dozen or so Brahmins were brought into Kodagu just to conduct services in the temple specially in Bhagamandala. But as years passed, their number increased, and the above mentioned short story of Chandra Varma and shudra kanni in skanda purana together, convinced the Raja that Amma Kodavas are inferior in status and took over the priestlyhood status in Kodagu temples. From then Amma Kodavas lost their priestlyhood status in Kodagu, it seems.

After crossing centuries of dark years, in November 1834 some Arruna Kodavas donned the sacred thread at Balmberi (Balamuri) on the banks of the river cauvery. They became followers of the Brahmin monastry (matha) in Ramachandrapura in Shimoga District in Karnataka state. In 1847 the head of this monastry sent them instructions as to the rituals they were entitled to perform. Amma Kodavas from Queggattnaad who had not donned the sacred thread in 1834 did so a few years later at the Irpu temple under the auspices of the monastry at Kaanuur in Udipi in Dakshina Kannada. Sometime afterwards a few Amma Kodavas who still remained unattached to a monastry became diciples of the monastry at Subramanya in the Dakshina Kannada District.

## 'URAALIS'

Uraalis are the primitive artisan tribes of Wayanaad of Kerala, being blacksmiths, carpenters, potters and basket makers. Among them most of the carpenters and potters families discontinued their traditional occupations became agriculturists by owning their own land on the line of jamma tenure. All these groups adopted Kodava culture including customs, rituals, traditions, dress and family names. They eat mutton, game meat, pork, but not beef, and drink alcohol. It is likely that they have entered to Kodagu during 8''' centure A.D. In Kodagu blacksmiths are called as Kollas, carpenters are called as Thachchairi, now Airis, among them another sub-group is Kambala Airis, who are regareded as outcastes, Potters are called as Koayavas, and basket and mat makers are called as Medas, and they act as drummers at the feasts.

The Medas live independently all over the country and subsist on the produce of their handicrafts, basket, mat, and umbrella making. It is their privilege to receive annually at harvest time from each Kodava house of their area as much reaped paddy, as they can bind up with a rope 12 cubits in length. They dress like the Kodavas, only in a poorer style. Their religion is the worship of Kaali and demons. The Medas live on rice, vegetables and animal diet, beef included. They are a quiet people, not robust in body and of a sallow brown complexion with black straight hair.

## 'KANIYAS'

It is also likely that Kaniyas came to Ammangeri during 8th century A.D. and settled there. Gradually some of them moved to other places of south Kodagu and a group migrated to Mangarouth (Mangaluru). Their original occupation was forttme telling (Astrologer). They also hailed from Malabar and are found in almost everywhere throughout southern Kodagu. Originally they were Malayalam speaking people, but gradually adopted to Kodava culture. Kaniyas used to fix the auspicious timings for conducting religious ceremonies of the Kodava house or Vakka or village or Naad, hence they were being respected. The Kodavas used to pay for this service of the Kaniyas in kind once a year, some measure of paddy called 'Uumae'. Gradually they too became agriculturists.

Other castes who have settled in Kodagu during 17th and 18th century A.D. are, Heggadaes, Bunts, Maleya, Bannas, Binaepattas, Kaavadies, Thulu Gowdas, Lingayets, Brahmins, Gollas, Baaniyas, Kukkaas, Baadagas, Theeyas, Nayars, Vellas, Kaapalas, Maraathaas, Marthaas, Kurubaas. These communities were immigrants from Malabar and Mangalore area during the period of the Lingayet Rajas. Most of them except Brahmins and Lingayets have adopted the Kodava customs and language.

## GOWDAS IN KODAGU

The Gowdas are quite a big community in Kodagu. They are mainly cultivators and herdsmen. They are settlers from the regions below the Ghats in Dakshina Kannada district. It is probable that Gowda community people through the sea route came from East of Mediterranean sea area to Indus Vally and settled there for some centuries and are herds men.From there one group moved to Agasthya region (south India) on the western coast line and settled in Dakshina Kannada district as herds men and gradually accepted agricultural occupation.

Two other groups moved from the Indus Valley region towards the Eastern side of India and settled in the Gowda Desha, a part of present Bihar state. From there crossing Vindhya mountains moved to the Agasthya region, one group settled in Andra Pradesh and the other group settled in Karnataka (Karnata). Andra region people speak Telugu language and Karnataka people speak Kannada language. Whereas Gowda people who have settled in Dakshina Kannada region having close contact with Tuluvas (Tulu language speaking people, believed have migrated to Mangalore region from East part of Africa) who speak Tulu language, gradually some of the Tulu words, because of cultural diffusion, mixed with Gowda language and gradually became Half original and another half aliean that is tulu language. So people started to call that language as Arae bhaashae.

During 18th century the sanguinary and relentless persecution of the people of Kodava by Tippu Sultan and the deportation of a large number of them to Srirangapattana resulted in a decline in the population of Kodavas.

The Lingayet Rajas too were said to have exterminated whole families of people suspected of treason against them.

"Wilks's account is that, in order to open a direct route to Malabar, Haidar suddenly invaded Coorg, and offered a reward of 5 rupees for each head brought before him. After about seven hundred rupees had been paid for he was struck with the handsome features and relented, ordering the decapitation to cease," (page number 283 last para-Imperial Gazetteer of India-Mysore and Coorg-by B.L.Rice-1908)

In 18th century, Dodda Veeraraja Odeyar, Raja of Kodagu made attempts to bring people from outside the District and encouraged them to settle in Kodagu by granting them lands free of assessment for some years and on low assessment during the subsequent years. Between 1799-1808 from Dakshina Kannada District Amara sullya, Puthoor, Kasaragod, Subramanya, Manjeshwara, Kumbala, Bantwal and nearby areas from every village brought 15 members and made them to settle in Kodagu.

Among them some are Tulu Gowdas, Hegdes, Baniyas, Bants and others. To these people Raja gave the jamma properties of the Kodavas which were left without Successors and the property after Massacre of the Kodavas by Tippu Sultan, giving the same family names with two objectives- one is to raise revenue and the other is to increase the strength of the ?ghting force. Through this process other caste people got family names in Kodagu. For every man whom Raja brought to Kodagu presented a kuppya, sash and a turban and made it mandatory to wear them, and also inducted some of them to his army. Tulu Gowdas are largely found in Padilaalaqnaad and Yedaenalaqnaad of Madikeri and Virarajapete taluks respectively.

The Vokkaligas of Mysore region called Negila yogis have maintained their identity for over a thousand years. They have existed as a separate class from the time of Gangas of Taikad. Among them main sub-groups are Gangadikara, Morasu, Hallikara and Nonaba. These groups are mainly settled in Somwarpet Taluk areas.

The Gowdas worship Venkataramana swamy to whom they make offerings once a year in September. They also perform ancestor worship and they belong to 18 clans namely— Nandra, Bangara, Hemmana, Kabar, Mulyra, Chalyara, Barasanna, Setti, Goali, Gowda, Kabura, Lingayet, Gundana, Chithara, Karamber, Devara, Nayara and Saale.

In the year 1934 after the meeting of Amma-kodavsa at Balamuri (Balmberi) Tulu Gowdas of Kodagu arranged a meeting under the chairmanship of Nuddyamanae Sri Mandappa the then sessions judge of Kodagu and in that meeting unanimously they have rejected to wear the Kuppya, sash and Mandaethuni (which the king ordered to wear) and decided to wear during marriage a white coat, white jari bordered kachaepanche and a silk shawl on the shoulder, that is they have returned to their traditional dress from that date.

## CULTURAL HISTORY OF KODAGU

Culture denotes refinement of mind and manners. Culture is the soul of the people, the basic beliefs, attitudes and spiritual values which have become their way of life. It is a source of both mental delights and physical comforts; it makes one forget the crudities of the external world; it creates a refined taste; and more than everything else, Kodava culture enables a Kodava to harmonise differences. Customs are generally accepted conventions which 1 are put into practice consistently and devotedly, and those practices gradually become a part and parcel of what is called culture. Cult or cultivate, is an act of development, a conventional process, an individual or social discipline etc. Rituals observed, system of worship, traditional values, manners, social conduct, language or dialect, a certain pattern of customs, names erc, form different roots and branches of the tree-called culture. Similarly, songs, hymns, classics and all kinds of literary" out-put are scripture.

The people of Kodagu have evolved a distinctive culture through the ages. The Paat style in poetry is the unique feature of Kodava literature. Kodavas had inherited culture and were endowed with refined tastes right from their birth. There is no need for them to go abroad to acquire culture. Kodava Paat holds a mirror to life. There can be no better means of understanding the mind of people than a careful study of their words, idioms and proverbs. The culture of the Kodavas enables them to practice simple piety, to honour parents and elders, touching their feet thrice, to tolerate religious diversity, to lead a life of virtue and to give much with grace - Balliya manaslue maapmaadi. The Ain-manae, Ambala, Mand and Parmb were centres of cultural activity. Noble principles were imbibed along with the mother's milk. The mother's advise to the child "Construct tanks, sink wells, plant trees, cultivate the land, wipe the tears of the af?icted and protect your followers and country. (as soon as a Kodava woman delivers a male child, a burning ball is shooted towards the sky fixing it to the bow and arrow, after introduction of gun culture, a gum is fired in the air to announce his birth, then a bow and arrow made from the veins of a castor plant is placed in the baby's hands, symbolic of the martial traditions of the Kodavas)

The most part of the history of Kodaga are in the form of "PAAT style"with complete picture or story of the event or person or deity. Some of such PAAT are 1) Deshaqatt paat, (description of the land and how it was administered.) 2) Kaaveri paat, (the story of Kaaveri) 3) Thott paat(lullabies) 4) Makkada paat (Nursery Rhymes) 5) Battae paat, (song for the way) 6) Mangala paat (wedding song) 7) Nari Mangala paat (song for Nari marriage-after killing a tiger) 7) Chaavu paat ( funeral song) 8) Polchhi paat, (song in praise of the dead person from birth to death and praying the God to send the dead persons soul to heaven) 8) Devada paat (songs of Gods and Goddesses) 9) and songs of Heroes.

Kodava culture like other societies consists of Proverbs, old sayings, riddles, beliefs and superstitions. There are more than 760 proverbs.

Kodava folk-arts, folk songs and dances came out of the hearts of those simple people in natural way of the day's gone-by. These folk —arts such as songs, dances, fables, and ballads left by the ancient poets who lived within their own small environment, are still admired and held in high esteem. During ancient and medieval period Kodavas did not know to read and write and were out of the literary world, and indeed Kodava language had no script.

In those yet unrecorded manners of speaking of the ancestors, one could see the wealth of wisdom and knowledge of people who expressed or sung them extempore. What had thus begun in the hoary past, were passed on for generations in unconventional ways, That is our rich intellectual heritage. In their traditional festivities, weddings and social and religious ceremonies or celebrations, one could still find a lot of well-thought — out ancient precepts and practices prevailing. They sang the song of the universe; they prayed for the humanity and they worshipped Mother- Earth. They also knew about the stars and planets, and many more things without even going to an elementary school. Their knowledge was admirable. They knew about the seven seas and seven continents and fourteen worlds. They knew about the illusive heaven and hell. These things together enriched Kodava lives, human values and ethics.

These are the people, the Kodavas, who fostered a way of life for centuries, living away in the hillside and plains as hunters and agriculturists. They had and still have their own traditional dress, very colourful and dignified. The Kodava race is after all a part and parcel of India's ethnic mosaic. Their folklore too carry the same views and spirits of what those elsewhere in India had said and sung, but the art and beauty of the folklore of Kodavas lie in its abundant charm, originality and profound melody. Whatever their functions or ceremonies the song (baalo paat) begins thus;

Baalo. .. baalo. . . nangada. . .
Deva..baalo. . . Madeva. . ..
Devi... baalo. .. Madevi. . ..
Patta. . . baalo. .. Suuriya. . .
Kuuda. . .baalo. . .Channuura. ..
Bhuumi. . .baalo. . ..]abbuumi. ..

All the kodava ballads begin with these words, and those are symbolic of their noble sentiments and poetic rituals. Every aspect of the Kodava folk—songs seem lovely because those lines depict simple truth in a flowing style. Whatever experiences they had, spoke out in the form of songs from the depth of their hearts. They seemed to have been very much accomplished individuals. From line to line they blurted out the song without any prior thoughts or notes, revealing their intellectual prowess. All ballads of Kodavas may be related to festivals, wedding, death etc. and this continues in a greater detail till date. What is interesting to note is that the song flows effortlessly, often spiced with beautiful similies and aptly used idioms in just a dialect that was spoken by hardly one lakh and odd people. The Kodava fimeral (chaavu paat and polchi paat) song is certainly poetic and philosophic from beginning to end., with beautiful similies and metaphors the song inspires every feeble heart, and the poetry is true to life. Kodava folk-songs consists of a good many worldly truths, and those words and rhythms freely collide as the cane sticks clatter all over the Kodagu horizon.The big-bang drums, the blowing of trumpets and pipes, the clattering of the cane sticks, all fill the air, and throughout the jungles and fields, hills and dales of the land that was once a home of exclusively the Kodavas for many centuries.

The folklores, folk-songs and folk-dances are generally thought- provoking. There's nothing that could be ignored in these nor considered as insigni?cant. Those spontaneous pioneers who created the wealth of folklores, folk-arts, dances etc. were certainly the greater thinkers greater than the modern men and women who seem to be intellectually bankrupt and super?uous. In that way those anonymous creators of these folklores and folk-arts live longer and for generations in the hearts of people. At present some folk- arts and folklores are recorded, but some are not because they are out of mind and out of practice.

# Some of the Place Names in Coorg:
# A Linguistic Analysis

*- Dr. Lalitha K. P.*

## ABSTRACT

This document gives a thorough Linguistic Analysis of Place Names in Coorg (Kodagu), a district in Karnataka state, India. In this paper an attempt has been made to trace the changes that have occurred in the place names of this district due to various factors which include geographical location of the district, influence of the languages of the other states and districts sharing borders with it, perceptions of the Non-Kodava speakers like Kannadigas, British etc. The Analysis of the place names of Coorg has been described and a discussion about the changes with relevant examples has been presented.

**Keywords:** Coorg, Kodagu, Kodava Language, Dravidian Languages.

## 1. INTRODUCTION

Need is the source of every innovation. Language is the medium discovered by virtue of basic human need which separated us from the other species. A medium discovered to express our feelings naturally is a reflection of our cultural and social life and the geographical environment in which we live. The rise of villages is also a major phase of human social progress. The names of villages of places are the footprints of the human steps towards civilisation. These place names contain social, cultural, historical and geographical information about the human life. We can conclude that the language that was discovered as a basic tool for communication and the place names given based on the experiences are inter-related and therefore the linguistic analysis of place names is vital. The 'village' is to society, like what family is to an individual.

# 2. DESCRIPTION

## 2.1. The analysis of place names in the district of Coorg is described as follows:

The place names of Coorg district have their own unique character in the background of language. Geographical boundaries of the Coorg district also play a vital role. The place names were influenced by Malayalam language from border of state of Kerala, Kannada from Hassan district and Hunsur taluk of Mysuru district and Tulu from Dakshina Kannada district. 'Kodava' language, being a member of the Dravidian language family has influences from other Dravidian languages as well. Also, major languages of the lineages of the rulers who ruled Coorg over time, English of the British and the languages of the tribes such as Yerava, Kuruba etc. have made their own influence on the place names in this district.

## 2.2. Generic list of place names of Coorg

The linguists have studied the place names by dividing them in to two groups, viz. 'specific' and 'generic'. Here both 'specific' and 'generic' are separate syllables. When these syllables join, the tones vary at some places.

The generic structures seen in the ending of the place names and their brief description are as follows:

**Some Generics**

| | | | |
|---|---|---|---|
| 1. | Ooru | 2. | Keri |
| 3. | Okkalu | 4. | Pura |
| 5. | Mangala | 6. | Gaala |
| 7. | Godu | 8. | Koppa |
| 9. | Kote | 10. | Yeri |
| 11. | Pete | 12. | Kunda |
| 13. | Guppe | 14. | Maadu |
| 15. | Nadu | 16. | Kattu |
| 17. | Badaga | | |

### 2.2.1. Ooru

This is the original Dravidian term which indicates places of living. Naadu, Grama, Sanna, Pattana, Tode, Nedu. [1]

According to Mr. M. Chidanandamurthy, there is proof [2] from inscriptions that some names which end with 'ooru' were formerly the names ending with 'Pura'.

Ooru: Place of living, an inhabited Place – a Village, a Town, a City. [3]

Since this is a Dravidian term, this is used in Kodava language with a slight difference. For example:

Nalluru (Kannada) Naloor (Kodava)
Kirugooru (Kannada) - Kirugoor (Kodava)
Kanooru (Kannada) - Kanoor (Kodava)

Ooru is used in the 'Kodava' language with a change of u > y sound. We will see the merging of vowel sounds when 'specific' and 'generic' merge. For example, Hosa + ooru > Hosuru.

### 2.2.2. Keri

It is a word that indicates the places of living. Beedi, Angadibeedi. [1]

The meanings for beedi given in the Tamil dictionary are – group of houses, village etc. [4]

For example:
Nadikeri
Shettigeri
Parakatageri
Konanjageri
Aiyyangeri
Biligeri
Monnangeri

---

However, in Kodava language, 'Keri' means a geographical unit smaller than village. Villages were formed due to merging of several Keris. Example, Nalkeri.

The change from 'ga' sound to 'ka' sound results in 'keri' to 'geri'.

This is also the place of living for the people who perform their secondary occupations. Example: Shettarakeri – Shettigeri

Nayinda (barber) keri – Nadikeri

### 2.2.3. Okkalu

Actually, 'okka', is a term in Kodava language that has become 'okkalu' in Kannada. In Kodava language 'okka' means family. For example, a place where forty okkas or families live. Each okka (okkalu) or families have their distinctive names. These are called 'manepeda' or 'okka peda' (In Kodava language, peda means *name*). Example: Kolera, Kallichanda etc. These are called Kolera okka, Kallichanda okka etc.

### 2.2.4. Pura

It is a word that indicates the place of living (Sanskrit word) – Town, house, city.[3]

It is used widely in all parts of India In all Indian Languages or of all generic of Sanskrit. It is used to mean simply a village or Settlement. For example, a place or town where a community called 'siddhas' lived: SIDDAPURA.

### 2.2.5. Mangala

Though Mangala is similar in meaning to Sanskrit term called "Brahmanara Agrahara" in Kannada, the forms such as mangala, mangila, mangli are used in other places too, where Agraharas or Brahmins are not present.

The scholars associate these names to Chola connection. However, in the context of Tulu place names, this association doesn't hold relevant. According to R. K. Manipal, the meaning of the term is non-Sanskrit in origin and similar to Prakrit, where the term denotes a place abundant in watersheds and a place fertile for sowing.[5]

Mangala means "An agricultural track or a fertile country. Mangala is used as a Geographical nomenclature."[6]

"The term Mangala as it occurs in the place name Mangaluru is interpreted by some scholars to mean a fort or a protected place. In the case of place names where the term Magala is attached to a Dravidan suffix of prefix, the term may be taken to imply an agricultural tract or a fertile country.[7]

The above logic and comments of the scholars also apply to the place names in Kodagu district. The local languages belong to Dravidian language family. The influence of 'Tulu' language and culture were also prevalent on this taluk. Here also, chances of seeing the Brahmin Agraharas may be less. Similarly, the generic 'mangala' indicates presence of abundant watersheds and the appropriate place for sowing.

### 2.2.6. Gaala

This is also the short form of 'mangala'.[8]

According to the inscriptions, 'mangalas' are the places or villages donated to the Brahmins. This started from the reign of Cholas. It is possible that the village names that end with mangala may be the villages that were donated to Brahmins. There is a proof that Cholas ruled at some places of this taluk. For example, Kannamangala (Kandangala).

### 2.2.7. Godu

It is a word which indicates the geographical features. It means mountain, tower, hill etc.[1]

Meaning: Hill, top of the hill.[3]

It is used as 'godu' due to shift from 'ka' sound to 'ga' sound.

Kodu: It means a horn, a tusk, a bunch, a branch in Telugu. It is used in the sense of rivulet also. But in Kannada it signifies a point, a peak or top of a hill. [9] For example, Karadigodu – The hilly area with dense woods where bears take refuge.

### 2.2.8. Koppa (Koppalu)

Koppalu - Small Village, a Hamlet.[3]
Koppa(lu): Chikkahalli, kaloor, community of huts. [3]

Koppalu means small village or place. For example, Gonikoppalu is originally Govinakoppalu, a place for cows (Govu), market for cows. A small area reserved for the trade only, the features seen in the common villages were not seen in this area.

### 2.2.9. Kote

Nirmanavachi – compound built for the defense of the military, strong compound walls.[1]

Kote: Fort wall or the wall protecting the city or village (a fort, a wall round a town; a rampart). Example: Chennaihana kote, the area ruled by the Palegar Channaih.

### 2.2.10. Yeri

It is term with origin in Malayalam. 'Yeri' means dense forest area. Example, 'Puliyeri' means the highlands where tigers take shelter or a dense forest appropriate for the living of the tiger.

### 2.2.11. Pete

It indicates the places of gathering of the folks, commercial centre or place of business. It is a place of selling the crops grown on the surrounding agrarian areas and purchasing the materials from the distant places.

### 2.2.12. Kunda: Parvata Soochi

'Kittel' has given the term 'a piller of bricks', pillar made of bricks for the word 'kunda'. The term 'kunda' in Kannada denotes hill, mound etc. In Kodava language, the term 'Kunda' clearly denotes 'hill'. Kodava language has the influence of Malayalam and 'Kund' means hill. In Malayalam also, 'kunda' means hill. This point has been clarified by field data also. Example, Belagunda (Bilugunda).

### 2.2.13. Guppe

Kuppa, Kuppe, Guppe, Koppas have the meaning of Guttu, gumpu, guddu etc.[8] Example, 'Rudraguppe' means the place of the group of Rudra and his other devaganas (angels).

### 2.2.14. Maadu

High lands, rooftop.[10] It is a name of the place which is geographically taller than the outer areas. 'Maadu' also means roof top or sky. For any place, sky is the roof.

### 2.2.15. Nadu

These nadus were seen during the rule of local chieftains (Palegaras) and during the Hoysala rule. Example: Bottiyat nadu, Shreemangal nadu etc. These were the places under the ruler ship of some palegaras.Even 'Manusmriti' refers nadavas. It means nadus were present even during the time when this edict was written. In Tamil, 'nat' means village. The places where people lived were called nadus. In the Taluk here, the 'nadus' were formed with merging several ooru and keris.

### 2.2.16. Kattu: Kettu (Kodava)

Which means round, obstruct, restrict etc.[1] Example, 'Pathkettu' a place where pattukoota ghosts have been restricted and quarantined.

### 2.2.17. Baadaga

Though this term means small village, R. C. Hiremath takes the reference of Kittel dictionary and says that it could be padu>padi>badi>vadi (da). [11]

In support of the following view, there are terms in Tamil dictionary such as padi, padai which mean village, base of the military. – (V. Gopala Krishna Linguist for many languages)

In his work, the poet Pampa said, 'Aidubadamam Avargeevudu' (five villages should be given to them); according to the reference made by Sham. Bha. Joshi, the patch of these nadus is nothing but bada. Though, for Pampa, a warrior himself, it is possible that he may have referred to giving military bases as well.

In the context of the names of places in Coorg district, 'Badaga' means 'military base', since there are many villages with 'badaga' in this district. All of these were seen in the places which were in direct control of the kings, Paleyagars.

## 3. DISCUSSION

### Linguistic differences occurred in few place names in Coorg

Due to various reasons including the ease of use, frugality, pride of the natives about their culture, or the influence of Kannada which remained the language of trade, inappropriate pronunciation by the British, we may witness with the current status of the place names of the district undergoing phonetic changes, assimilation, word elongation, apostrophe errors, unnecessary consonants and use *mahaprana* etc. This resulted in the changes such as constriction of meanings, extension of meanings, disintegration of meanings, improvement of meanings, changes in meanings and wrong meanings over the time; the current status of usage is the result of this metamorphosis.

## 3.1. The names of the places which have undergone phonetic changes

The changes in phonic sounds are called phonetic changes. These phonetic changes occur due to human nature of frugality.

### 3.1.1. Changes in 'ha' > 'a' Phones

Hatturu>atturu

Therahalu>Teralu

### 3.1.2. Consonant 'va' > 'ba' Change

Veeranani>birunani

Veeranga>beeranga>beeruga

### 3.1.3. 'pa' > 'ha' Change

We can see so many changes of consonant 'pa' to 'ha' during the time of Keshiraja, author of 'Shabdamani Darpanam'. According to his own words –

"sanda 'pa' karakke 'ha' karam
 dorekolgum vikalpadim samyogam
 sandhisidode dushkaramadu
 sundara ma deshiyinda membar vibhudar
 vrutti - karnataka shabdada 'pa' karakke vikalpadim
 ha karamakkum
   dvitvadol piridum pa karakke 'ha' karamilla, idu deshiyol chelvu". [12]

Palanda > halugunda
Pudukkeri > hudikeri
Peggala > heggala
Pathakett > halligattu
Pachchat > hachchinadu
Poldur > hodduru

### 3.1.4. 'ga' > 'ka' Consonant Change

Gottigeri > kottageri

### 3.1.5. 'ta' > 'da' Change

Kavati > Kavadi

## 3.2. Some names where mahapraanas (aspirated) changed in to alpapraanas (unaspirated)

Therahalu > Teralu

Hakattooru > Akatturu

## 3.3. Few place names which have undergone Assimilation

When our voice organs are stressed, a tone can be corrupted in to another form or a tone can be shifted to closer tones which are similar in pronunciation. This is called assimilation.

Aranji > Arji
Kalatmad > kaltmad
Arakeri > Arkeri
Karamad > Karmad
Chennangi guddadooru > Chennangi gudluru
Kukkaruru > Kukluru
Nala-keri > Nalkeri
Mareyooru > Marur
Biliyooru > Bilooru
Bengeyooru > Benguru
Moorudhare > Maldare
Moorukallu > Moorkallu
Mekeriyooru > Mekooru
Mahakoota > Makutta
Yedeyooru > Yadooru
Bolumad > Bol-mad
Hadiyooru > Hadooru > Hatooru

## 3.4. Few place names which have undergone changes in Meaning

If a name of the place has been changed in the usage and records in to a different form to give meaning which is entirely different from its origin, it means the place name has undergone meaning change.

The terms, which have had their origins in the Malayalam and Kodava languages, have lost their meaning when they have been translated in to Kannada and retained with different meaning in both the records and usage. Also, the influence of the British English and wrong pronunciation has also resulted in the changes in the meanings of the place names. The meanings of the names of a few places have been constricted due to loss of original meaning, meaning has been lowered, extended, bettered at some places as observed during the place name studies.

Examples –

- **Nayinda keri > Nadikeri**

The origin of the name was in the barbers called Nayindas. However, over the time, has changed to 'Nadikeri', which means *'Central Hamlet'*.

- **Kadanoorandur > Kadanur**

The place name was in use, in association with the close aide of the devaganas called 'Kadanoora'. However, today's form of 'Kadanoor' means *'Place of Battle'*.

- **Bollooru > Bellooru**

In Malayalam language, 'Bolla' means *'Water'*. However, today, 'Belloor' is used as *'White Village'*.

- **Kakotu Acchayyana parambu > Katotu Parambu**

The place is named after a person called Kakotu Achahyya. The present form, Kakotu Parambu has lost the name of the person.

- **Chennangi guddadooru > Chennangi gudluru**

The earlier name Chennangi Guddadooru was indicative of the village which is closer to the hill. Today it is called as 'Gudlu', which simply means *'hut'*.

- **Nellooru > Nallooru**

In the Kodava language, 'Nel' means *'paddy'*. However, 'Nalla' gives different meaning, which means *'good'*.

- **Karadi gudde > Karadi godu**

In Kodava language, 'gudde' means a *'collection of something in huge volume'*. However, it is used as 'Godu', which means *'Highland'*.

- **Mailadi > Maithadi**

In Kodava language, 'Mile' means *'Peacock'*. The term was derived from Malayalam to Kodava language. However, the place name 'Maithadi' is meaningless.

- **Pathkett > Haligattu**

Originally, the place name 'Pat-koota' was a symbolic *'Place for Ghosts'*. The Kannada form of 'Haligattu' means *'A Group of Villages'* is a severe distortion of the original meaning.

- **Konda kere keri > Kondangeri**

A name of a village which has a hamlet or village containing Konda kere *('pool where someone was murdered')* is now turned to 'Kondangeri' – *'a Hamlet of fire'* (Konda means fire).

- **Kollepete > Palibetta**

The original name from 'Kolle' refers to *'Hunting'*. However the place name was changed to 'Palibetta' by the British.

- **Govinakoppalu > Gonikoppalu**

The place name referred to *'cows'* ( Govu means cow). But today it's changed to 'Goni', which means *'Sack Bag'*.

- **Ponnappanapete > Ponnampete**

The name referred to a person called Ponnappa. Now it is changed to 'Pon' which means *'Gold'*.

- **Poldur > hodduru**

In the Kodava language, 'Pold' means *'Festival'*. 'Hodduru' is a corrupted Kannada form which resulted in losing the original meaning of *'a Village of Festivals'*.

- **Bolmad > Bollimad**

In Kodava language, 'Bol' means *'Empty'*. However, the corrupted form, bolli means *'Silver'*.

## 4. CONCLUSION

The above illustrations show you how the place names were changed in phonetics and meanings in both usage and records to corrupted forms due to eased use in pronunciation and perceptional errors of the native Kannada and English speakers.

# REFERENCES

[1]   Sirigannadam Arthakosha, p. 68, 134, 340, 141, 88.

[2]   Chidanandamurthy M., Vaagartha, p. 15.

[3]   kannada.kannada.English.Nigantu. p. 116, 256, 204, 150.

[4]   Kelavu Deshanaamagalu, p. 372.

[5]   Sthalanaama Adhyayana Hege? Eke? R. K. Manipal, Sthalanaamagala Adhyayana, Lekhanagala Sangraha, Sampadakaru, Prof. D. Lingayya, Dr. Chekkere Shivashankar, p. 11.

[6]   Studies in Indian Place Names, Vol. XV, p. 98.

[7]   Studies in Indian Place Names, Vol. XV, p. 112.

[8]   Edegalu Heluva Kamnada Kathe, Sham. Ba. Joshi, p. 144.

[9]   D. J. Gow, A Study of Village names of Mysore District, p. 141.

[10] Kannada Ratnakosha, p. 57.

[11] Place names in Karnataka – KUJH Vol. - V June 1968, p. 97-98.

[12] Keshiraja Virachita Shabdamani Darpana, Sam D. L. N., p. 173-174.

[13] Sakaleshapura Parisarada Sthalanaamagalu, M. Vishwanath, p. 121.

[14] Krishna Bhatta Sediyaapu, Kelavu Deshanamagalu, Sahityasangha, Manipala, 1965, p. 372

# WORKS FOR REVIEW


1.  Dr. Vishwanath, **Graamanaamagala Parivesha**, Devi Prakaashana, Mysore, 2000.

2.  Prof. D. Lingayya, Dr. Chekkere Shivashankar, (E), **Sthalanaamagala Adhyayana,** Lekhanagala Sangraha, Karnataka Janapada Parishat, Bangalore, 2008.

3.  Dr. K. Kempegowda., **Kannada Bhasha Swaroopa**, Kannada Adhyayana Samsthe, Manasa gangotri, Mysore.

4.  M. Chidanandamoorti, Dr. Chidananda, **Samagra Samputa – 1**, **Kannada Shasanagala Samskrutika Adhyayana**, B.C. 450-150, Swapna Book House, Gandhinagar, Bangalore.

5.  M. M. Kalaburgi, Dr. Marga, **samputa – 2**, Swapna Book House, Gandhinagar, Bangalore.

6.  D. N. Krishnaih, **Kodagina Itihasa**, Prasaranga, Mysore University, Mysore, 1974

7.  Hampa Nagarajayya, I. Ma. Muttanna(Pra.Sam.), **Kodava Kannada Nighantu**, Kannada Sahitya Parishattu, Bangalore.

8.  Baragooru Ramachandrappa (Pra.Sam.), Upasamskruti Adhyayana Maleya Pustakagalu, Kannada Sahitya Academy, Bangalore 1993.

9.  Kannada Adhyayana Samsthe, **Ephigraphiya Karnatika**, Mysore University, Kodagu Jille Samputa-1, 1972

10. Sangamesha Savadattimatha, **Dravida Bhasha Vyasanga**, Roopa Rashmi Publishers, Kalburgi, 1990.

11. M. M. Kalburgi, **Kannada Naama Vijnana,** Swapna Book House, Gandhinagar, Bangalore 2010.

12. Raghupati Bhat, Kemturu, **Hesarallenide**, New Star Publications, Bangalore, 1989.

13. K.V. Narayana (E), **Sthalanaamagalu, Parivartane Mattu Prabhava**, Kannada Vishwavidyalaya, Hampi.

14. M. Nanjayya, Honganooru, **Sthalanaamgalu,** Prachara Pustaka Maale, Prasaaranga, Mysore University, Mysore.

15. Sham. ba. Joshi, **Edegalu Heluva Kamnada Kathe**, Madhava Ballala Bandhugalu, Dharawad, 1847.

16. M. Chidanandamoorti, **Bhasha Vijnanada Moola Tatvagalu**, D.V. K. Moorti Prakashana, Mysore.

# NIGHANTUGALU

1.   Kittel Kannada English Nighantu
2.   Samkshipta Kannada Nighantu
3.   Kannada Ratnakosha
4.   Igo Kannada Nighantu
5.   Kannda Kastoori Kosha
6.   Webster English Dictionary
7.   Dravidian Etymological Dictionary
8.   Mysore University Kannada English Nighantu

## BIBLIOGRAPHY

| | | | |
|---|---|---|---|
| 1 | A History of Kodagu | 2012 | P.S. Appaiah |
| 2 | A Tiny Model State of South India | 1953 | Muthanna I.M. Poly Betta, Coorg |
| 3 | A Mannual of Coorg- A Gazetteer | 1870 | Richter G. Delhi |
| 4 | Archaeology of Coorg | 1978 | Subbaiah K.K. Mysore |
| 5 | A Study of Village Names of Mysore District | | Javare Gowda D. Dejagow Trust, Kalanilaya, Jayalaxmi Puram, Mysore-21 |
| 6 | A Study of the origins of Coorgs | 1997 | K.C. Ponnappa |
| 7 | Coorg Memoirs | 1855 | Moogling H. Bangalore |
| 8 | Coorg and the Coorgs | 1931 | Muthanna Pandanda |
| 9 | Coorg District Gazetteer | 1965(Ed) | B.N. Satyan, Bangalore |
| 10 | Coorg Land of Beauty and Valour | 2010 | P.T. Bopanna |
| 11 | Dateline Coorg | 2000 | P.T. Bopanna Rolling Stone, Publications, Bangalore |
| 12 | Discover Coorg | 2008 | P.T. Bopanna, Prism Books Pvt. Ltd. Bangalore |
| 13 | Epigraphia Carnatica | 1914(Ed) | Rice Edn. Revised, Vol.I Coorg District |
| 14 | Epigraphia Carnatica | 1905 | B.L. Rice, Vol. IX |
| 15 | Ethnographical Compendium on the Castes and Tribes found in the province of Coorg | 1887 | Richter G. Bangalore |

16  Ganapathy B.D.                        1980      Kodavas, Madikeri

17  Indian Chronological Tables           1977(Ed) Dr. B.S. Kulakarni,
                                                    Karnataka University

18  Kodavas                               1980      B.D. Ganapathy, Jyothi
                                                    Prakashana, Temple Road,
                                                    Madikeri

19  Kodava English Dictionary             2010      Ponjanda. S. Appaiah

20  Mysore and Coorg Gazetteer            1878      Rice Lewis B.Vol.lll ,
                                                    Bangalore

21  Nugets from Coorg History             2008      C.P. Belliappa Rupa & Co.

22  Phonology of Kodagu with              1976      R. Balakrishnan
    Vocabulary                                      Annamalai University

23  Souvenir Centenary of                 1998      Bar Association Virajpet
    Celebration Virajpet Courts                     Kodagu 1968 - 1998

24  The Coorg Tribes and Castes           1948      Krishna Iyer L.A. Madras

25  The Coorg Memoirs                     1971      Muthanna I.M. Mysore

26  The Romance of Indian Coffee          2011      P.T. Bopanna,
                                                    Prism Books Pvt. Ltd.
                                                    Bangalore

27  Victoria Gowramma                     2010      C.P. Belliappa Rupa & Co.

28  Dravidian Etymological Dictionary

29  Kodava English Dictionary

30  Deccan Herald (Sunday Spectrum)